Rosalie Roos, from a daguerreotype made by
S. F. Beurling in Havana, 1855

TRAVELS IN AMERICA
1851–1855

by
Rosalie Roos

Based on
Resa till Amerika 1851–1855
Edited by
SIGRID LAURELL

Translated and Edited by
CARL L. ANDERSON

Published for
SWEDISH PIONEER HISTORICAL SOCIETY

SOUTHERN ILLINOIS
UNIVERSITY PRESS
Carbondale and Edwardsville

Copyright © 1982 by Swedish Pioneer Historical Society
All rights reserved
Printed in the United States of America
Edited by Catherine Moutrey
Designed by Quentin Fiore
Production supervised by Richard Neal

Library of Congress Cataloging in Publication Data

Roos, Rosalie, 1823–1898.
  Travels in America, 1851–1855.

  Translation of: Resa till Amerika 1851–55.
    1. United States—Description and travel—
1848–1865. 2. Roos, Rosalie, 1823–1898.
I. Anderson, Carl L. II. Laurell, Sigrid, 1895–
III. Title.
E166.R7313   973.6'4'0924 [B]   81–187 MY 3 '82
  ISBN 0–8093–1018–X   AACR2

CONTENTS

ILLUSTRATIONS

ACKNOWLEDGMENTS

The Swedish Pioneer Historical Society and the Nils William Olsson Research Fund supplied welcome assistance with expenses, and I am grateful for information and advice kindly provided by Mrs. Sigrid Laurell, Professor H. Arnold Barton, Mr. Kermit B. Westerberg, Mr. William McGowan Matthew, and members of the very resourceful staff of the William R. Perkins Library at Duke University. Miss Helen Anne Fuller and Miss Ruby Bailey typed the manuscript expertly. My wife, Jean Bradley Anderson, deserves special thanks for a close reading of the manuscript and many helpful suggestions for its improvement.

Durham, North Carolina   —C.L.A.
September, 1980

PREFACE

On 20 October 1851, just four months after the Swedish novelist Fredrika Bremer had left Charleston, South Carolina, for the last time and returned to the North to resume her tour of the United States, a traveler also from Sweden but unknown outside her family and small social circle disembarked at the same city, not as a celebrity making a tour but as a frightened young woman looking for work. When Rosalie Roos sailed home four years later, she could not claim to have matched Miss Bremer's achievement of three volumes of letters from America (*Hemmen i den Nya Verlden* [Stockholm, 1853–54]; *Homes of the New World*, 2 vols. [London and New York, 1853]), but she had nevertheless compiled a voluminous record of her experiences in the many letters she had written to her family in Sweden. The letters were forgotten for many years after her death in 1898 but were discovered recently by her granddaughter and extracts were published which, in translation, make up the contents of the present volume.

Sweden in 1851 was on the eve of a social and economic upheaval that by the end of the century was to take it very far along in its transformation into the affluent, cosmopolitan industrialized state that it is today. Rosalie Roos's decision to break away from the constraints to which she thought she had been doomed in Sweden and to try her luck, if only temporarily, in America is a small but very revealing episode in the history of that transformation, which sometimes created severe strains for the individual in the course of the dislocations in family and community life and the eruption of new standards and values that took place throughout Sweden.

Rosalie left Sweden with decidedly mixed feelings. Her strong sense of family ties and of allegiance to her homeland was combined with a painful realization of how stifling Swedish life had in fact been for her. Her formal schooling had ended when she was fifteen—no more had been available to girls. While at home tutoring her brothers for admission to higher schools, she had toyed with the possibility of turning her interest in ideas and her aptitude for languages to good and profitable use but had got no further than to compose some inconsequential verses inserted by one of her brothers in a Göteborg newspaper. The only prospect remaining to her had seemed to be marriage, but that too was blasted when at the age of twenty-seven her long engagement to a pleasant but evidently ineffectual young man terminated with the collapse of his career in a brokerage firm and his flight to Hamburg and thence, presumably, to America. It was an outcome that her father, to her chagrin, had all but predicted. Rosalie saw stretching before her the typically wan lifetime of a nineteenth-century spinster of good family, spending her days in an endless round of social calls and other inane pursuits occasionally interrupted by duties performed as somebody's maiden aunt. As an unmarried woman she would be dependent by law and custom then prevailing in Sweden on the good will and perhaps even the charity of others. To these probabilities, then, America suddenly presented itself as a desperate, even if temporary, alternative.

As it turned out, America marked the great turning point in her life. She discovered that in America, despite its reputation for paying little heed to fine social distinctions, she could earn her livelihood without loss of dignity—an important first step toward personal independence. She learned also that her self-esteem and usefulness to others need not be jeopardized or curtailed by what still seemed then to be certain spinsterhood. And not least, she became convinced that her vision of a better life for women than social convention and law yet permitted was not impossibly daring after all but entirely feasible, only requiring for its ultimate realization the energy and direction that she, for one, was now prepared to devote to it.

Two years after her return to Sweden she married, and the once-feared prospect of spinsterhood passed out of her life forever. If she felt thereafter that she had to give priority to the care of her family—she had four step-children and two of her own—or to temper her crusading spirit in deference to the sensitivity of her husband's position in public affairs as a member of the Supreme Court, she gained through marriage a degree of mobility not yet accorded unmarried women. She was prepared to make as full use of it as possible, having so keenly savored independence in her years in America.

She soon began to be actively engaged in many kinds of reform having to do with women's higher education (a paramount concern), nursing care, the care of retarded children and the deaf, housing for working people, and the legal and social status of women. At the close of her life she was recognized as having been, with Fredrika Bremer and Sophie Leijonhufvud, "one of the three pioneering women and leaders . . . who transformed social and economic conditions for Swedish women."[1] She wrote frequently for the newspapers—pseudonymously, so strong still was the prejudice against the appearance of ladies in print—but her principal contribution of this kind was no doubt her joining with Sophie Leijonhufvud in the founding of "Magazine for the Home" (*Tidskrift för Hemmet*) and coediting it with her for the first nine years. The magazine was conceived as a means of giving women at home ready access to the world of ideas. It was modeled on the reviews and magazines—in particular, the newly started *Harper's New Monthly Magazine*—that had supplied Rosalie with such instructive and useful reading in America that she had vowed she would continue reading them in Sweden.

As Rosalie's letters from America quickly reveal, she was, like many another foreign visitor, amused, puzzled, or dismayed by many of its customs and mores. However, one subject—slavery—presented her with more than ordinary difficulties of interpretation, and it is necessary to consider her dilemma briefly. It was the publication of *Uncle Tom's Cabin*— that "scandalous libel" as it was immediately called in the South—that obliged her to break discreet silence and protest doctrinaire attacks on what she had supposed was her invincible conviction that slavery was wrong. She held fast to that conviction, to be sure, yet she was now also obliged to acknowledge there were complications she had not foreseen. She was witness to none of the mistreatment of slaves as Mrs. Stowe described it, and certainly nothing like the brutal beating of two servant boys in her own home in Sweden that she had noted with disgust in her diary. She was a spectator, apparently without embarrassment, of the subservient position assigned to the blacks and of the humiliating money games, for example, that they were bidden to play at Christmas; but again, she had herself seen no evidence of physical cruelty—on the contrary (to her surprise), much that seemed to attest to their contentment. Accordingly, she found herself in the uncomfortable position of wanting at one and the same time to remain true to her convictions and yet be fair and accurate in her observations. And, genial person that she was, she also wanted to be as much at one with her Charleston "family" as possible.

The problem was exacerbated by her having happened to arrive in the South just when the slavery debate was entering its most heated phase—nowhere more than at Charleston—in the decade before the outbreak of war. From the early, often apologetic justifications of the economic need of slave labor on the plantations, the proslavery forces had by the 1850s begun to turn to a variety of defenses against the increasingly

---

[1] Eva Fryxell, "Rosalie Olivecrona," *Dagny* (1898), p. 1.

harsh attacks on the slave system coming both from the North and from within. Rosalie heard a fair sampling of these arguments. In one of her letters she disparages the frequently repeated claim, usually drawn from biblical evidence, that slavery was of divine origin or at any rate had divine sanction and could therefore be expected to persist into eternity. It was not a theory she could credit, yet the complication here for her was that someone like her kindly employer and friend, Mr. Peronneau, openly subscribed to it, an admirably hardworking manager of his home and plantation as her letters describe him, one who might well think of himself and his fellow planters as patriarchs charged with the responsibility under God's plan of presiding over the well-being of his family and of his "people."

Closely related to this position was the argument that slavery in America offered the African Negro both material and spiritual advantages he would otherwise not have. This was linked in turn with another old argument that slaves in the South were better off than the poor of other countries.[2] Rosalie had to concede that she knew of tenant farmers in Sweden who were treated much worse than the slaves she had seen; benevolence, then, appeared not to be unknown to southern paternalism. The argument took a "scientific" turn when extended in the ethnological defense definitively made by Dr. John Bachman, with whom she once rode the train to Orangeburg. He was well known in Charleston as the genial and learned pastor of the Lutheran Church and internationally known for his collaboration with Audubon in natural history. His theory, elaborated in *The Doctrine of the Unity of the Human Race* (Charleston, 1850), was that slavery in America was advantageous to the African Negro through providing him with the opportunity to step out of the misery of thousands of years spent in tropical jungles toward his restoration as a full-fledged member of the human race. What was now required was the active regard by Christian churches for his spiritual health and advancement; as Rosalie might have observed, the churches of Charleston were in the 1850s intensifying their response to these obligations.

Yet another proslavery argument then current was the Aristotelian class theory of slavery as a necessary means of freeing talented and creative members of society from time-consuming menial labor.[3] Rosalie never tied this theory to frequent observations in her letters of the "aristocratic

---

2 William S. Jenkins, *Pro-Slavery Thought in the Old South* (Chapel Hill, 1935; rpt. Gloucester, Mass., 1960), pp. 73, 211.

3 Jenkins, pp. 286–89.

attitudes" of South Carolinians, but she herself, let it be said, had ample opportunity to enjoy some of its benefits, especially in Charleston despite her position as governess;[4] they were indeed not unlike those she had known in her home in Sweden where servants belonging to a servant class attended to many of the family's needs. Although the theory was repugnant to her on moral grounds as a defense of lifelong servitude, it was yet at not very great variance from a mode of life she had been reared in. Given, then, the complexities of the issue in its workaday setting and the self-contradictions she began discovering in herself with respect to her formerly unassailable abhorrence of slavery, she thought she had good reason to deplore in her letters the superior tone taken in the criticism of southern attitudes toward slavery and other matters that she found in Fredrika Bremer's *Homes of the New World* when it appeared in 1853.

It is perhaps not surprising that when years later war had broken out between the states, she is said to have expressed herself in private conversation in Stockholm as being in favor of the continuation of slavery, an exceedingly unpopular stand to take in liberal circles in Sweden.[5] There is no doubt she detested slavery as strongly as ever, yet she apparently was still sufficiently moved by the recollection of her years in South Carolina to reject war and perhaps any sort of precipitate action as a solution to the perplexed human situation she had been in effect part of—unlike Fredrika Bremer, who had come to the South as an observer and student, and then had gone her way.

In her writings, Rosalie continued to have only scorn for theories she had heard in America of the positive good of slavery. On several occasions when pleading for improved educational opportunities for Swedish women, she did not hesitate to draw parallels between such theories and arguments then being advanced for keeping women "for their own good" within the confines of the home. She berated those who employed such arguments:

> You do as the slave owners do who extol the happiness of their slaves. "They have," they say, "the clothes, the food that they require; in case of sickness they receive the care and medicine they need; in their old

---

4 A position shown in the letters as not having excluded her from family life. According to a novel that Rosalie believed gave an accurate picture of the South (see p. 82, below), even the word "governess" was to be avoided. "This honourable name is not popular in America. I think we speak of them as young ladies who *stay* with us to teach our children" (p. 31).

5 Sigrid Leijonhufvud, *Sophie Adlersparre (Esselde): Ett liv och en livsgärning* (Stockholm, 1922), p. 112. Rosalie's remark is reported without explanation or comment.

age, when they can no longer work, they are nevertheless cared for; their lives pass in this fashion as free of care as can be, far freer of worry than ours, for we have to think about and provide for them." You speak in much the same manner; but as little as the slave owner would want to change places with his slave, just so little are you willing to exchange your condition for that of women. If you were to sit in judgment on yourselves, you could not in good conscience deny that your sophistries have as little worth as those of which the planters of the South make use in order to defend slavery. They say further: the Negro is of an inferior race . . . ; it would be futile to try to raise him up to the educational level of the Caucasian race. . . . What do you say to this, my lords who preach abolition, you who are so zealous for your black brothers' emancipation on the other side of the ocean but are pleased to offer these same reasons against loosening the fetters which you have so highhandedly placed on Swedish women?[6]

Rosalie employed the same strategy to the same end in a magazine article written two years later. She wrote then that assertions "that women are far happier in their ignorance than when they attain a higher development of their minds" have as little merit "as the slave owner's assurance that the condition of the slave is far more enviable and more carefree than his own."[7]

Rosalie's impatience in America with Fredrika Bremer's indiscretions and lofty philosophizing was supplanted on her return to Sweden by enthusiastic support of the arguments for women's rights erected in Miss Bremer's novel *Hertha* (Stockholm, 1856). The novel was described by its author as "the first fruit of the marriage in my soul of the spirit of the New World with Swedish conditions."[8] It depicted the intolerable dilemma in which a highly gifted woman of mature years is placed by the law, which permits her neither to marry without her father's consent nor to inherit property bequeathed to her by her mother that would make her independent of his rule. The novel included passages citing the freedom allowed women in America, a point that Rosalie could warmly corroborate. At first her friend Sophie Leijonhufvud shrank before the vehemence of the attacks in the press on *Hertha*, fearing the damage such a reaction would bring to the cause of women's rights itself, but she was won over

---

6 "En ropandes röst i öknen," *Aftonbladet*, 30 March 1857. This was one of a series appearing on 28, 30, 31 March and 1, 2 April that is mentioned later in this preface.

7 [La] St[raniera] (pseud. for Rosalie Olivecrona), "Om qvinnans intellektuella uppfostran," *Tidskrift för Hemmet* 1 (1859), 181.

8 *Brev*, ed. Klara Johanson and Ellen Kleman (Stockholm, 1912–20), III, 379.

by Rosalie's vigorous defense of *Hertha*'s arguments for reform that she published in a memorable series of newspaper articles in the liberal *Afton-bladet* in 1857.[9] Two years later the two women began publication of *Tidskrift för Hemmet*, their magazine for the home.

Yet another consequence of Rosalie's American experience may be seen in her attacks on the complacent acceptance in Sweden of a "refined education" as being best suited for women. When she wrote in this connection of the lack of good, well-trained teachers as a principal weakness of many girls' schools,[10] she was no doubt recalling misgivings she had felt in America regarding her own competence as a teacher, given the limitations of her education, and regarding the uncertain value of the kind of education she saw her American pupils had been expected to benefit from. At other times, when she criticized the typically narrow Swedish curriculum for girls, she could refer approvingly to the inclusion in the course offerings in American girls' schools of such "masculine" subjects as Latin, mathematics, and physics.[11] The school in America she knew best was of course Limestone Female High School, but she also had the example of the Reverend Legaré's Female College at Orangeburg and perhaps also of other schools, like the Lincolnton Female Academy near Spring Hill, where she had been a guest in the home of her friends the Hammarskölds. Her awareness of the efforts being made in these schools and those in England to raise the standards of education for women and of their deficiencies and occasional triumphs, had given her a basis for framing cogent arguments for the major reforms she fought for in Sweden.

The present volume is based on the Swedish edition, *Resa till Amerika 1851–55*, edited by Rosalie Olivecrona's granddaughter, Sigrid Laurell (Stockholm: Almqvist & Wiksell, 1969), but omits a brief account of an excursion on the Göta Canal taken before Rosalie's journey to America and abridges the notes of her travels after she left South Carolina, these being largely concerned with the route she took from New Orleans to Chicago and New York. For the benefit of American readers who may not be familiar with Swedish life and culture or who may not be familiar with antebellum South Carolina, I have supplied explanatory notes and have modified and supplemented Mrs. Laurell's commentary from time to time. I have tried to render the Swedish of Rosalie's letters and diary into idio-

9 See n. 6, above.
10 [La] St[raniera], "XXVIII—En af dagens frågor," *Tidskrift för Hemmet* 5 (1863), 263.
11 "Om qvinnans intellektuella uppfostran," p. 190.

matic English while keeping as close to the original as possible. This has meant, for example, retaining incomplete or loose constructions and other signs of hasty writing, but I admit to having made concessions to English usage for the sake of clarity.

Portions of Rosalie Roos's letters from America have previously appeared in translation in *Swedish Pioneer Historical Quarterly* 10, no. 4 (October 1959): 127–40 (excerpts of letters to Rosalie's brother-in-law translated by Nils William Olsson under the title "Rosalie Ulrika Roos in South Carolina . . . ") and were drawn upon by Montague McMillan in her *Limestone College, A History* 1845–1970 (Gaffney, S.C., 1970), pp. 55–63; and in H. Arnold Barton, *Letters from the Promised Land: Swedes in America* 1840–1914 (Minneapolis, 1975), pp. 62–68.

—C.L.A.

TRAVELS
IN
AMERICA
1851–1855

THE PERONNEAU FAMILY

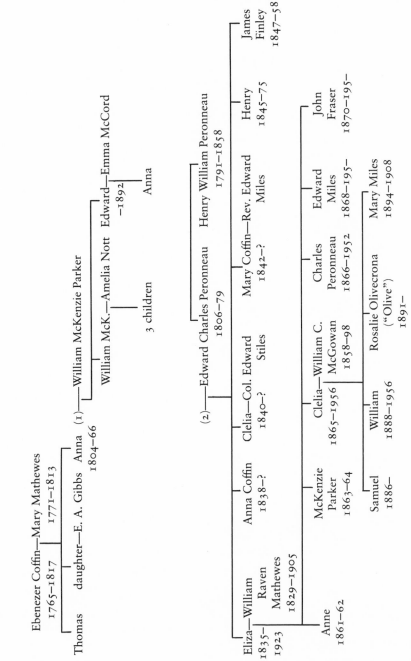

I

EARLY DIARY ENTRIES AND LETTERS

Rosalie Roos was born in Stockholm 9 December 1823. Her father, Olof Gustaf Roos, was an official on the National Board of Commerce. Her mother, Ulrika Euphrosyne von Keppel, came from a family said to have emigrated to Sweden from Livonia via Finland. Rosalie was the eldest of nine children, but the three who were nearest to her in age died in infancy. Her mother was not the timorous creature Rosalie's letters rally her for being, but a robust, outgoing woman of immense practical abilities. She attained the venerable age of ninety-five years.

Decidedly liberal in his views and an avid reader, Roos was determined to give his daughter the best education available. She was first sent to Maria Magdalena Schenson's boarding-school, located in Stockholm during the years 1828–36. When the Wallinska School[1] opened in 1831, Rosalie was accepted as a pupil in the first grade although she had not reached the required age.

In 1838 the Roos family moved to their newly acquired estate "Sjögerås" in the western province of Västergötland, and Rosalie's formal schooling came to a close. Instead, it was now she who began to teach her younger brothers and sisters and to devote herself to some of the domestic virtues, but "lest the mind be neglected" her father's well-stocked library was made available to her. She greatly missed her father, who was obliged to spend long periods in Stockholm on business and in seeing to the construction of a house on property his wife had inherited. Rosalie found diversion in long rambles in the woods and fields surrounding "Sjögerås," and she eventually acquired a quite respectable knowledge of botany, a subject in which her father had probably been her first guide.

Except for occasional verses, Rosalie left no records of her life before

---

[1] Founded by Anders Fryxell under the sponsorship of Archbishop J. O. Wallin; described in later years by Rosalie as having been the first step taken in Sweden to liberate education for girls from rote learning of the rudiments of religion, history, geography, and handwork. "Om behofvet af intellektuel uppfostran för qvinnan," *Tidskrift för Hemmet* 1 (1859), 6–7.

1843. A rose-colored diary bordered in gold carries the date 1841 on the cover, but the first entry was made 5 February 1843. "I have no friend my own age with whom I can share my thoughts and feelings, and I often feel a need to do so; I will therefore confide in you, but you must not make fun of me, as perhaps many would do."

Probably no friend can wholly take the place of a young girl's diary. On the other hand, it can easily give a somewhat distorted picture of her days since principally her cares and disappointments are likely to be confided to it. Nevertheless, Rosalie's sixty-five closely written pages also contain a great deal about her daily life and happy times spent with the neighboring families of Forsselius at St. Bjurum, Tham at Dagsnäs, Trolle at Skår, and Hall at Skara, where there were dancing, charades, and music as was the custom in great houses in Sweden in those days. Besides the instruction she gave her brothers and sisters, Rosalie's share of the daily chores consisted of much sewing and, at times, of weaving. We hear a sigh of relief when a lot of thirty-six handkerchiefs has come off the loom!

In later years Rosalie was to recall how, at a very early age and on her own, she reacted strongly to her insight into the dependent status of women and their inequality with men. The poverty she witnessed in the surrounding countryside gave rise to the written expression of such thoughts—for the first time in the little rose-colored diary. "Often when I see poverty and misery it breaks my heart that I cannot offer a helping hand, but must suppress the outcry in my heart because there is nothing that I can do. . . . Oh, if only I were rich, but as it is, I am a woman, and men in their pride do not permit women to act according to their own notion and feeling for what is right. It is surely barbarous, as though women did not possess as much good sense and discrimination as do men."

Her strong native sense of justice had undoubtedly been nourished by the writings of C. J. L. Almqvist, a prolific poet, novelist, and journalist whose advanced views on the equality of the sexes had made him the center of stormy controversy in Sweden. The newspaper *Aftonbladet* to which he contributed found its way to "Sjögerås," but Rosalie was familiar with his other work as well. When in the early 1840s she was thinking of ways of earning money in the future from her own efforts, she had ample opportunity to observe in newspaper advertisements how limited the possibilities were for women if they remained unmarried. Yet a marriage without love solely for the sake of securing an income seemed to her unthinkable.

On 19 February 1843 we read that Rosalie, along with her parents, had been invited to a baptism in the Trolle family at Skår. "I hurried so to finish my black silk dress for the occasion, and Johanna declared that I looked like a bride in it. Bride! No, that I shall never be, but no matter, for it is often the first step to a host of sorrows and worries that need never trouble those who are unmarried. I shall never be in love, I think, nor will anyone feel that way toward me; I am too ugly and too poor, and it is only beauty and wealth that entice fickle gentlemen." An entry a few weeks later nevertheless reads: "We danced ourselves into a frenzy last night. What fun it is to dance. . . . The men were quite merry. I danced every dance; there were ten françaises, five waltzes, and a cotillion."

At the end of February the sleighing was good and Rosalie's father set off for Stockholm. On 9 April she wrote to him: "When we returned from Skara, I found a letter from you; you want me in my letters to discuss a topic in order to make our correspondence more interesting; you named as examples fidelity, infidelity, marriage, friendship, good sense, pleasure, etc. That is too difficult for me, it is beyond me, but to oblige you, Papa, I chose the easiest—that is, friendship—and tried seeing what I could do with it. We shall see what you think of it." Unfortunately we never get to hear his opinion; only a very few of his letters have survived.

16 April: "This week has abounded in unpleasantness. For one, Thilda came in and told how Jonsson had beaten two of the boys so mercilessly that blood splattered up on the loomstead door. I was both terrified and angered and did not know really what to do; I cannot abide people who fight, they fill me with real loathing; ugh, they might as well be Russians. I took no notice of Jonsson nor spoke to him; I could scarcely remain silent, but Mama forbade me to say anything."

3 May: "Easter Monday, when we were at Bjurum I got a letter from you, my dear, beloved Papa, which made me profoundly happy. We danced and played charades. . . . I have been baking several times now; it is lots of fun, and no doubt will improve when I have learned to manage the dough a little better."

21 July: "I never have time to write down things here; how the time flies, and with every vanishing moment we are taken all the nearer to our final goal here on earth—and later, eternity. Oh, what labor, striving, and yearning we endure for the relatively short time we have to make our way here toward what lies ahead. . . . When life is regarded correctly, how strange does this struggle not seem, almost absurd! Nevertheless we go on just as strenuously as before. Such a myriad of contradictions in human nature!"

30 July: "Interruptions, constant interruptions break in always upon the moments I wanted to have to myself to pour out my thoughts. Oh, I do not know how people are able to fear solitude, fear their own society,

because for my part I am almost at my best then. If I had a friend to whom without fear of censure or ridicule I could divulge all my thoughts, perhaps it would not be so, but where is such a one to be found? I am now reading [Bulwer-Lytton's] *Zanoni*; oh, how I do enjoy it, no book recently has made such an impression on me; it speaks so directly to my own heart. Say what you will about these 'sketches of everyday life'[2] which are now so much the vogue—and it is true, they often are true and natural, one recognizes the setting in which one is constantly moving about, but how often does that life not seem trivial?—one longs for something higher, something more uplifting, for the little tasks of everyday life submerge the heart in a kind of apathy toward everything else and then it is refreshing to have the mind stimulated by something bright, something idealistic, that rises above our petty concerns. I am no hopeless romantic; preserve me from despising the quiet tasks of domestic life, from underestimating the housewife's humble yet high calling, the felicity of which consists in that of those about her, whose happiness——the girls are on their way in, I must stop."

21 August, four months before Rosalie's twentieth birthday: "Many happy, many sad moments have again flown by, flown away never to return, and every day one grows older and so I must for always say farewell to youth, its castles in the air, its shadowy play of the imagination, and its joys and its faith in mankind. Yet this time has been so short, I feel as though I were just a child, and now—now I will soon be so old. But it is such a bore to think about old age, for even if one could have everything in life one desired, life would not have the joy, the radiance, which belongs to youth; and then to be alone, abandoned by everyone, parents, brothers and sisters, oh! heaven preserve me from growing old . . . I would be so pleased to be allowed to die at any time now. I have, to be sure, many faults to correct, but maybe I will become worse instead of better, for the longer one lives the more one errs; we must flee to the mercy of our Maker and pray to Him not to call us too strictly to account, for who then could defend himself? I am in such poor spirits today, my eyes fill constantly with tears, I think myself so inferior to everyone and it is very painful. It would be grand to be pretty and happy and jolly, one would then be popular, but I am ugly, I am serious and quiet by nature, so no one really cares for me, . . . I feel that everything is such a burden and yet that everything changes and at another time I feel that perhaps my present thoughts are childish, even foolish—"

2 The title given to Fredrika Bremer's first three highly popular novels of domestic life (1828–31).

4

The autumn went by without leaving a trace in the diary. The next entry was not made until 21 January 1844: "Where have these days, weeks, and months disappeared to? Everything in my past life seems like a fleeting dream; can it be possible that I have lived twenty years, . . . I am no longer a child . . . and yet I feel that I am that still. Oh, I longed to leave the flower gardens of childhood! My liveliest wish was to become and to be treated as an adult, and now that I am that, I look back with sadness on the years gone by. . . . But away with all fears for what the future may hold! With eyes looking straight ahead and with firm resolve I shall go forward, convinced that in applying myself to the tasks ahead I shall win the strength to bear them."

Both excited and disturbed by her plans for the future, the twenty-year-old Rosalie, thinking in the first instance of her pen, began to feel her hopes rise that with its help she could make herself financially independent. For as long as she could remember, she had scribbled verses in celebration of special occasions within the family; and ever since she had come to know the joy of moving about freely in the woods and fields at "Sjögerås," she had given voice to her happiness in short poems. But how was she to know if her wings would keep her aloft? She had no one of whom to ask advice. Looking ahead to the autumn when a tutor was to take over the education of her two brothers still at home and she would have more time to devote to her own interests, she decided to ask for professional advice and made an interesting choice of consultant: none other than Love Almqvist. After weeks of waiting she received at last near the end of August a reply thanking her for writing and apologizing for the long delay. Almqvist modestly discounted his ability to advise her on such a delicate subject as she had broached with him. He himself, he wrote, did not share the prejudice of many men against women authors, but he could speak from personal experience of frustrations that lie ahead for anyone wishing to pursue a literary career. He wondered if she would have the courage to endure the unpleasantness and the bitterness of being misunderstood, and perhaps even of being abused. It was a warm, friendly letter but not one likely to have encouraged Rosalie. She left no record of the impression it made on her nor of her reaction to it, but years later, after she had returned from America and once again thought of a literary career, she remembered Almqvist's warning.

On 7 January 1846 she made what was to be her last entry in the little diary. Worried still about the future, she now had reason nevertheless to feel that the coming year might be a turning point in her life: "Does love really exist in this world? Is it not merely a beautiful poetic fancy, one of those castles in the air which collapse the instant they are touched? Is

there really a genuine love independent of outward appearances and——
but hush, I cannot clothe my thoughts in words. Is it possible that I am
his beloved? I have asked myself this question many times and have answered it affirmatively, but dare not put my faith in it. It may be merely an
illusion, a passing fancy, . . . And in any case, even if it were real, it is
nevertheless only a dream which never, never can come true. I do not
know myself what I feel, what I think, and in this case do not even wish
to inquire too closely." It was her brothers' young tutor, Pehr Eric Gjers,
who had so unsettled her, but it was not until the beginning of summer
that he and Rosalie reached an understanding. He was a personable young
man but without means of his own. Too extravagant a fondness for society
had obliged him to interrupt his medical studies at Uppsala and accept the
post of tutor. Botany being at that time a subject of study in medicine, he
no doubt was able to supply Rosalie with whatever she wanted to know
on that subject. But above all it seems to have been literary interests that
brought them together. Pehr was still present at "Sjögerås" during the fall
of 1846 in order to help prepare Emil Roos for admission to the military
academy at Carlberg in Stockholm for training as a naval officer. Rosalie's
older brother Axel was already in Stockholm studying engineering. On
her shoulders rested the responsibility for schooling her youngest brother,
Gustaf, who seems to have had little of the devotion to learning shown by
his elder brothers.

A year later, Pehr was employed in a brokerage firm in Göteborg in
hopes of putting his affairs in order and eventually of attaining financial
independence. In reply to a letter, Rosalie wrote to him for the first time
on 29 January 1847. "My Dear, Beloved Pehr! There, I have said it. . . .
But I don't understand how it is, it is as though I were too shy to call you
by your name; probably it is because I have never heard anyone say your
name to you[3] . . . but I shall get over this childishness! Thank you for the
sweet name you give me. It is the loveliest thing I can imagine to be your
'guardian angel.' May I always be that." Their separation, she went on to
say, had become painful at times: "Oh, if only we were not imprisoned
like this, separated from each other like this. . . . Sometimes I am so calm
and patient, but then there are times when I think that everything is so

---

3 Apparently Pehr had been addressed in the Roos household in the third person only,
perhaps not even by his surname but by his occupational title of *informator*. Rosalie follows
similar etiquette in letters to her mother and father, never using the second person pronoun,
not even the familiar form *du*, but referring to them always as "Mama" and "Papa" and
"she" or "he," though no less affectionately for that. This usage, not the least unusual in its
day in Sweden, has been translated in this volume into corresponding polite usage in English
under similar circumstances.

dreadful, dark, unbearable." She had been writing fiction, wishing that she too might help with their future responsibilities so that he need not bear the full burden of them alone. She had received her mother's permission to write to him, but space was limited and she had so much to tell him!

In August 1847 mother and daughter spent several days in Göteborg, where the two young people arranged for Pehr to spend Christmas at "Sjögerås." As the holidays approached, Rosalie's excitement mounted. "Oh Pehr, when I think that next week, next week the hour will strike when we shall be reunited, then I am all smiles and my imagination far outruns reality—may the latter catch up with the former. I <u>can</u> not, I <u>will</u> not believe it will be otherwise. So I shall not write much today but will <u>save up</u> and <u>save up</u> so that my lips will speak instead of my pen though perhaps forgetting a great deal as usual."

A year later differences had arisen that moved Rosalie to state opinions that evidently were not in complete accord with those of her friend: "Perhaps I should say a few words now on that subject which we undertook to discuss, but I do not think that our thoughts will coincide in this case. Has my Friend, who has previously shown himself to be fairly open-minded as to the kind of influence that women might have, now defected to those who have determined upon a definite limit beyond which women may not extend their activities, and who commonly restrict them to the kitchen and the workroom, that is, to handwork or sewing? Among those areas which men have usurped as 'belonging to their proper sphere of activity' is also, I suppose, the writing profession, for which reason those women who have dared make a career of it and become their rivals have been met with derision, shrugs, censure and have been obliged to fight step by step for every inch of the field of battle, which they perhaps have defended later on with honor. But this too is supposed to have something unwomanly in it, something 'mannish,' for just ask them, men in general, if they do not regard this kind of activity as exclusively theirs, if they do not look with a certain antipathy upon those women who encroach upon their rights.

"You are displeased with my wish that women be accorded the right to dispose of their property as they see fit; you believe that the changes in education which would thereby be required would eradicate 'the gentle, the womanly, in her nature.' I do not think so. I do not think that the augmented studies which would then be required to broaden the base of her education, to improve her understanding, would have that consequence. A real, genuine, soundly based education can work no harm; it must serve to refine every higher sentiment and indeed to quicken it in the first place. How many do not believe that those women who have been

7

taught something more than sewing, knitting, and housekeeping are totally incompetent to follow their calling as women, that is, in the sense of being housewives. I am audacious enough to take the opposite view. I believe that this higher education, provided it has gone beyond the superficial, will teach women to have a better idea of their duties and also will permit a richer fulfillment of them. . . . In saying this, I have only wanted to express the thought that increased knowledge cannot deprive women of the gentleness, refinement, which you are so good as to attribute to them; the understanding is what is cultivated in the acquisition of knowledge; the heart is the seat of virtue, and for what reason would the cultivation of the former deprive the latter of its gentleness, goodness, purity? Could we not look upon these two as being brother and sister who grow up together without the advances made by the one hindering those made by the other, but on the contrary inciting them to competition?—I should have liked to write more about this, especially in defense of my views concerning the right of women to hold property in their own name, but do not have the time now; also I fear I may be wearying you. It is delightful to correspond with you on a subject which provides us with opportunities to exchange and justify our opinions and which, <u>if you so wish</u> , we shall continue in person or in next year's correspondence. Do not suppose, however, that I stubbornly cling to an idea once I have seized upon it; no, I wish only to set forth plainly my reasons for it and then let you rebut them and I will gladly go over to your side if I find your objections to be well taken."

Unfortunately we cannot follow the continuation of this discussion, for none of the letters to Pehr written during 1848 have been preserved. From that year, however, two letters, one to Rosalie from her father and one from her in reply, throw much light on the closeness of their relationship. During a visit in the summer to the island resort of Känsö near Göteborg, Rosalie had at last told her father of her friendship with Pehr. There seems to have been no immediate reaction on his part, but late in autumn Rosalie received the following letter, a vivid self-portrait of Olof Roos. Because fathers of that era have sometimes had to appear in the literature as uncompromising household tyrants, not least in connection with their daughters' matrimonial aspirations, it will be to good purpose to let a father of another sort be heard.

Stockholm
20 November 1848

My own girl!
Ever since your confidences at Känsö I have thought many times of

speaking a little more with you on that subject, which I confess left me at the time with a heavy heart. I would almost suppose it to be superfluous to engage in discussion with you concerning the importance of that step in which love is the first link; but my experience is not yours, and so I wish to state that if three-quarters of those who are married were to speak the unadorned truth, they would say that that step might well have been omitted. The bulk of them suffer in silence, paying for a delusion, content to be able to assign the blame to love, which has always been and remains blind. However much I enjoyed reading novels in my time, I cannot approve the tendency in most of them to take it as their purpose to reveal hardheartedness and insensitivity in parents who look with disfavor on their children's romantic attachments. At times this disapproval is prejudiced and without cause, but in general it has its basis in the purest source of parental love—affection and concern for the future welfare of their children. Why do a mother and father struggle and labor to provide a heritage and an education for their children if not in order to bring happiness to their future and to provide them with a more pleasant life than the parents many times have themselves enjoyed? May one and should one now take offense at the disapproval of this or that ill-considered connection that has been formed if an unimpassioned eye has discovered it will lead to misery? It can surely be assumed that a father's critical eye can discover faults where the loving eye of his daughter has only found perfection. It can surely be further assumed that whoever has experienced life's shifting fortunes in love as well as in that which comes after—married life—has a broader perspective on the future than the girl who has flown only on the wings of parental love within her own home. If you accept these assumptions, and I have never had other than the kindest and most loving thoughts with respect to you, surely you will admit that the judgment I pass on the subject does not emanate from some impure source, one seeking to make you unhappy, but on the contrary. I am sure you already know what my principles as to the matrimonial connection are, that A is not to be said before one can say B[4]—for seldom can there be happiness where the contracting parties must wait for each other for many years. When love is one's companion in wedlock, it extends its hand to friendship, to habit that becomes second nature; one grows accustomed to the bond which, say what you will, drives freedom, that precious freedom, out of doors. Where there has been long waiting, sighing, longing, love perishes, and when at last it is possible to build a nest, it is done more from a sense of duty than from inclination.

---

4 Cf. the German business proverb, "Wer A sagt, muss auch B sagen" (Whoever says A must also say B).

Life that begins with a certain chill often concludes in frost. If as so often happens, there are also financial worries, then say farewell to the little god. I therefore have no patience with those men who invite their partners to the "long dance" before the music is ready. That G. has done this to you is further confirmation of the flightiness which I fear marks his character.

To be sure, love comes like a thief in the night, but it does not usually gain admittance unconditionally, not even with the unwary. If there is not the appeal of money, there usually is that of spiritual or physical beauty. In my eyes, G. possesses none of these. He is a congenial fellow in company, with a small but pleasant singing voice, but he lacks the characteristics of a man of promise: decisiveness and perseverance. His life up until now, according to what he himself has said and others have confirmed, has been marked by vacillation, a disposition more for pleasure than for work. Although a poor boy, he enjoyed partaking of the wasteful pleasures of the rich; thereafter followed dejection and indebtedness. He is not wicked, for what he is reproached for is merely a consequence of thoughtlessness; but neither is he virtuous, that is, he does not rest on his own bottom, he is independent neither in his thinking nor in his actions. Such a one have I found him to be; I would that I were mistaken, for I entertain more good will than hostility toward him. Perhaps at long last a better spirit has awakened in him, and on the path he now follows he will vindicate himself, but it is still too soon to judge what lies ahead.

Do not suppose that I have the least objection to make to his poverty; that is readily overcome when thrift and resourcefulness are practiced. No, it is personality that will always constitute the subject of my inquiry. I myself have known what it is to be poor, managed to acquire assets, been threatened by circumstances with the loss of them, but always, even if I say so myself, reasonably thrifty, which helped me get ahead. I love to see the same thing in others.

I shall not believe you are afflicted with the weakness—the marriage disease—which typifies many a girl, who in order to avoid being called an old maid is ready to hold out her hand to the first one on the scene, for then you would little resemble your father, with whom you otherwise share some characteristics. It is my wish that good sense and pride will direct your footsteps—something of that sort has been my aspiration. But do not confuse pride with vanity; I consider the one to be virtue and the other to be folly. If it should be your fate not to share happiness with a good man, bear in mind the happiness of not having to share unhappiness with a bad one. Keep also in mind that, God willing, your father will leave you means enough, supplemented by those talents with which you are endowed through him, so that you may readily turn your single status to advantage. That status is so common in our country and in your family that there is by no means anything terrible in it.

I do not want to go any further in calling into question your taste, your feelings, and possible desire to be what in girlish parlance is called "being provided for." It is all natural enough; but given that footing of lovingkindness and confidence on which we stand with respect to each other, notice ought, to my thinking, to have been given long before. A well-bred girl who loves and honors her parents and in turn is treated affectionately by them, ought no sooner to receive a man's declaration of love when it is made with honorable intentions than to communicate it at once and obtain their advice or consent— for was it not at Känsö that the first word of this was spoken?

—But I will withhold any further reproaches, certain that your own feeling of what is right and proper makes them heavy enough, and to salve them I will only add that if your liking for Pehr G. continues even after the attention I have tried to call to his character and he continues to mend his ways and wins the public trust in which his fortune resides, I shall not, when the time has come, set myself in opposition to your happiness—but will pray to God that two temperaments that I consider to be unlike may fuse into one to the advantage of both. . . .

Tell me about your pupils. Do you speak with them in any foreign language? That is the best sort of practice, after all. I burn with desire to have the boys out traveling a bit. Greet them and all the others, from your

Papa

Rosalie's reply follows:

Sjögerås
26 November 1848

My good, beloved Papa,

I have to thank you for and answer your dear letter of the 20th, which now lies before me. That you have only my happiness in view, I well understand from the contents of the letter as well as from your treatment of me in other respects, and I acknowledge it gratefully, but I will nonetheless confess that this letter has hurt me deeply and cost me many tears. For that reason I want to reply to it at once and in writing because it seems easier to me that way than in person.

There is much, much I would like to write, but since not all my thoughts can be written down on this paper, I must make a selection, but it is not easy, for they crowd in on one another and do not fear, but clamor, to see the light of day. —You are displeased with me regarding the feelings which I divulged. This displeasure grieves me, indeed grieves me more than I can say, for if I could redeem myself with my life, with <u>my personal</u> happiness, then I should not for one moment have the least hesitation to sacrifice them. I have nevertheless sat in judgment on myself to inquire what my fault may consist in, and to that I can find no other reply than this: "I have given away my affection, as it were, my heart, the <u>only</u> thing in the world I could call my own without having to be granted permission to possess it, without egotistically calculating the advantages I would take from it." Is that then something so unpardonable, I have inquired of my conscience, but it has answered "no," and before God and before the whole world I am not ashamed to profess my love. To be sure, it is possible that I am wrong, that I do not correctly perceive what is right and wrong in this matter, and if so, I expose myself to punishment and suffering in propitiation of a fault that was nevertheless committed only in ignorance. You criticize G. for having expressed some of his feelings toward me though he could not make actual then and there the expectations he raised at that time. In this I must go to his defense, for there was in it no thoughtlessness and flightiness as you believe. That he could become attached to me, who possess so few of the outward charms which generally captivate gentlemen, shows at once that he is less superficial and flighty than most, for it gave witness to his placing greater value on the kernel than on the shell, which generally is more often of the first importance. He respected me, and that feeling gave rise in time to a heartfelt and sincere devotion which was not aired in meaningless words nor took the form of what is commonly called flirtation, neither in flattery nor hints, but only in cordial good will and a lively interest in everything concerning me. He said many times, not hinting at anything, but speaking in general, that he did not consider it right to join someone else's destiny with his so long as there were no bright prospects for the future, that there are occasions when it would be a duty not to express one's feelings. But a moment arrived when we openly admitted what we had each of us felt already, and for that I was as much the cause as he. Whether it was right or wrong only He alone knows who sowed the seeds of love in the human heart, but I do not believe that He took offense from it, for I prayed that I be punished if it were a sin. G. has reproached himself many times that he did not succeed then in holding his tongue, but the words once said could not be recalled. I thought many times: Can it be wrong to show true affection to one who extends its like to me? But I admit sincerely that I did not see it so. Had it been a question of courtship, a formal declaration, I agree it would have been my duty to refer the decision at once to those who were entitled to decide for me, but there could be no question of that for a long time to come. Since it was rather to be regarded as a friendship, I did not think for one moment that I ought to trouble my parents with such an avowal. I reasoned thus: We are pleased and happy in the certainty that both of us have in knowing that we possess an impartial friend, one who follows with genuine interest the other's fortunes; we cannot see ahead to what may lie in the bosom of time, but should the day come when we can be something to each other, and our thoughts are unchanged, only then would it be time to take the decisive step with our parents' blessings. No promise, no declaration binds us; we are in this matter completely free and our attachment to each other is based only on mutual inclination.

You say at one place, "To be sure, love comes like a thief in the night, but it does not usually gain admittance unconditionally, not even with the unwary. If the appeal is not one of money, it is usually one of spiritual or physical beauty. In my eyes, G. possesses none of these." I am much too unmaterialistic to be able to give away my affections for selfish reasons or to sell them; I have myself too little physical beauty to attach exclusive importance to externalities. As for the spiritual, G. is not lacking. It is true he does not possess the outstanding qualities of mind and heart which characterize a great man, but show me, my good Papa, one single person in our social circle who possesses this higher degree of spiritual beauty. I at least have not been able to discover it, and as highly as I also value it, I fear that it is fairly rare, and underneath the glossy varnish through which so many try to shine in the eyes of the world, a discerning eye discovers much meanness, self-interest, and selfishness, qualities which drag the soul down into the dirt, instead of lifting it upward toward its origins. I am not blind to G.'s faults, for in my mind love should be more clearsighted than blind since it looks on the beloved object with greater attention than others do and thus becomes aware of stains where no one else notices them. The difference lies much rather in the fact that whereas others criticize and condemn, it seeks with a soft touch to expunge and diminish them, and itself not being free of fault, does not demand faultlessness. I am aware of the careless and thoughtless mistakes G. has committed in his past life, and I hope precisely for that reason that he will not repeat these mistakes since he acknowledges and regrets them.

It was not until August 1849 that the engagement was announced, an event preceding which Pehr had written to Rosalie's father to obtain his consent. The letters from the following year reveal a Pehr who was often out of sorts as he made little progress in his job in Göteborg. Rosalie tried her best to cheer him up, analyzing sympathetically his various suggestions of trying another kind of work, assuring him that her own needs were small if only she could be sure of the constancy of his love. Once again she offered to help out by submitting fiction to a newspaper in Göteborg, but he still disapproved. She pleaded in reply:

"It is impossible for me to regard it as something shameful or disgraceful for a woman to try to earn whatever her abilities permit. A day may come when necessity will require it, and it can then be useful to possess resources and not be compelled to see one's work go unwanted. Perhaps you are afraid that I would overtax myself and thereby endanger health and eyesight. But as for that, be calm, my dear! I have learned to value both too much to put unnecessary strains on them. On the contrary, it would do me indescribable good. It would furnish me with an employment which not only interested me for the work itself and the results it would bring but which also diverted my thoughts and directed them away from the depressing subjects that so frequently preoccupy them while doing mechanical work with a needle. . . . Papa has such big expenses that he cannot contribute much to our household. What joy would it not then be for me if I did that! The realization would add considerably to my courage and my happy temperament, for now I am often dejected by thoughts of my impotence, my uselessness, so much the more trying since I know very well I lack neither ability nor strength."

In February 1850 Rosalie began once again to jot down sporadic entries in a small blue notebook:

"Often there comes over me a deep, inexpressible longing to have a friend to whom I could utter those thoughts which stir deep within my soul, . . . but these wishes are in vain. I will therefore entrust them to paper as I cannot and will not entrust them to anyone else. . . . When I am happy, I have many to whom I can tell of my happiness, but for my pain I have no one in whom to confide; it resides in the depths of the heart. . . . If I could sometime accomplish something useful for my fellow creatures, I could gladly go on living, but if I must always remain so powerless, so dependent, so tied down—oh, then let me be allowed to die!"

II

THE CROSSING TO AMERICA

Rosalie's relationship with her friend in Göteborg reached a crisis with the coming of the new year, 1851. More than ever his letters seemed to reflect despair at ever being able to establish himself in Sweden, and it had occurred to him that perhaps he should seek his fortune in America. Rosalie looked more realistically at such plans but added in a long letter dated 5 March: "If you see benefits over there which I do not know of, if you know of resources and prospects which are unknown to me, no thought, no consideration of me is to stand in your way. I cannot accompany you, help you, lighten your burdens, but neither shall I place any obstacles in the way of your happiness; I shall pray for you, that is all I can do."

Her last letter to him is dated Easter Eve, 1851: "Great gaps often occur now in our correspondence, but that is as you will have it. You know from before how I suffer because of it and now more than ever, so that it is not even worth mentioning. . . . That you are unhappy and weighed down by worries I see and know with all the greater sadness as I discern my own incapacity to relieve them in the slightest degree. . . . If you love me as I want to be loved, if you understand me as I wish to be understood, if you feel as I do, I shall be able to meet at your side every misfortune calm and contented."

That spring, entries once more resume in the little blue notebook, one in May revealing that Pehr had written on 16 May from Hamburg to Rosalie's brother Leonard in Göteborg appealing to him for aid in making his way to America.

24 May: "Bitter overwhelming moments, no not moments, but hours, days, weeks, have gone by since I last aired my thoughts here. In that time I have suffered more than I believed I could endure, I have undergone trials which I had thought impossible to survive. . . . The dream of my youth, my hopes of a happy, busy, fortunate future—all, all is at an end. At times my courage falters, I feel overwhelmed, devastated—it is as though I were half dead and a dull numbness turns to stone a heart that once beat so warmly. But my heart is not dead, only numbed, it awakens at times and beats just as strongly of anguish, of misery, of—oh, I can't name it all. . . .

I have much youthful strength, much youthful life left, though it is now
fettered and paralyzed, but now and again it raises itself up in all its
strength and shakes its shackles; it will not believe that all worldly bliss
has come to an end. . . . I must pull myself together and remember that I
still have responsibilities toward my fellow men."

In the difficult period that followed, Rosalie gave intense thought to
what shape her life would now assume. To stay on yet another winter at
"Sjögerås" where she would no longer be needed for the tutelage of her
brothers was unthinkable. Her parents were planning to return to Stockholm as soon as their house there was finished, and her sister Leonie,
engaged to be married to a young district forester, would likely take over
"Sjögerås."

Nothing would do but that she leave home and obtain independent
status, get additional schooling, and broaden her experience. By chance
she then heard that Hulda Hahr, whom she had met the previous summer
on a visit to Stockholm, had left Sweden in the fall with her brother Franz
for South Carolina. Brother and sister had obtained positions at a large
boarding school for girls, she to instruct in music, he in both music and
drawing. The news sparked hope in Rosalie. Her father had often said
that he would like to see one of his sons try his luck in the New World.
Rosalie hastened to write to Hulda Hahr to ask if she saw any possibility
for her too to obtain employment there. She received by return mail an
encouraging reply and had little difficulty obtaining her father's consent to
let her go; he looked on the broken engagement with relief, if anything,
and even if he had little understanding of his daughter's desperation, he
could allow himself highminded thoughts of her ability to build a future
for herself. It was no doubt more difficult for her mother to become reconciled to these far-ranging plans and not to give in to the disapproval
that friends and relatives had of so hazardous an enterprise.

Rosalie was later able to write: "With women, decision and action
are <u>one</u>—within three weeks everything was arranged for my departure."
Leonard in Göteborg and her father in Stockholm gathered information
as to which ships were scheduled to leave for Charleston. There were good
connections to New York, but it was rather difficult to ascertain how the
voyage would continue from that point.

Nevertheless, arrangements seem to have proceeded more easily than
anyone had dared hope. Even the problem of securing suitable traveling
companions for Rosalie almost solved itself, for a minister and his family
were setting out for South Carolina in the middle of August to serve a
little Swedish congregation at the iron works at Cooperville in western

South Carolina.¹ The works were managed by a Swede, Capt. Carl W. Hammarsköld, whom financial difficulties had obliged to emigrate to America with his family in 1849. He had a cousin living in Charleston, an architect named Hjalmar Hammarsköld, who happened also to be the brother of his wife Hedda. Hjalmar Hammarsköld had promised to meet the family and arrange for their journey inland. They were to make the crossing to America on the newly built sailing vessel *S. A. Lamm*, under the command of Capt. John Valley. Miraculously, Cooperville was only about six miles from Limestone Female High School, Rosalie's destination.

She arrived in Stockholm in good time, but the day before the scheduled departure the disappointing news reached her that the family she was to travel with would have to postpone their journey since one of the children had contracted scarlet fever. Rosalie's parents and Leonard, who had accompanied her to Stockholm, urged her to wait also, but she felt a strong inner conviction that she must not be dissuaded even if a crossing "in the pens and stalls" unaccompanied by the protectors a maiden lady should have looked far from alluring. There were no separate quarters for passengers sharing space between decks, but Leonard succeeded in persuading the captain to relinquish his cabin to Rosalie, incredible though that may seem, but from later remarks it appears that he had other quarters of some sort at his disposal.

(It was just as well that the minister's family did not set out as planned. Shortly after Rosalie's arrival in America, the Swedish colony at Cooperville was disbanded and Captain Hammarsköld left his post there. Differences among the employees seem to have brought about this sudden alteration. Hammarsköld moved to a small iron works in North Carolina which had been leased by his son Carl, but since their house there was very small, his wife Hedda lived at the inn in Limestone while waiting for an addition to be built. Their daughter Heddie was a pupil at the girls' school.)

On 16 August the *S. A. Lamm* weighed anchor and the following day reached Sandhamn,² where it was to be readied for the transatlantic voyage. Its cargo from Charleston would be either rice or cotton, and prob-

---

1 Cooperville, "the Iron Capital of South Carolina," one of many sites in western North and South Carolina where iron was mined and worked in the early nineteenth century. The industry had already begun to decline rapidly before Hammarsköld's arrival, for the richer ore and vast coal reserves in Pennsylvania made the wood-fired foundries and water-run forges of the Carolinas scarcely profitable. Bobby G. Moss, *The Old Iron District: A Study of the Development of Cherokee County—1750–1897* (Clinton, S.C., 1972).

2 A seaport on one of the outermost skerries in the Stockholm archipelago.

ably it took on cobblestones as ballast from Stockholm. At Sandhamn the captain was joined by his family, and the company passed the time waiting at the customs inspector's house. Rosalie wrote her first letter home 17 August 1851: "We are now lying at anchor at Sandhamn, and dinner having been consumed, I hasten to what is now my dearest occupation, writing to you. Yet my pen is little able to express what I feel, what I should wish to say to you! ... Now that the anguish of the hour of farewell has somewhat abated, I have returned to the impossibility of old of believing in the reality of all that has happened. I still think myself always the subject of a bad dream, as though I were walking in my sleep. ... We expect to be here for another four days, and in that time I can possibly receive messages or letters from you since pilots go back and forth nearly every day between Sandhamn and Stockholm. So write and leave your letters at Sundeman's grocery store at Jerntorgsgatan in Räntmästare House, where the Sandhamn people put up."

It becomes evident from Rosalie's description that a substantial parcel of food had been included in her extensive luggage. Her mother had prudently provided an abundance of rusks, hard tack, loaves of bread, butter and cheese, ham, preserves, wine, and black currant juice "which soon committed the nuisance of fermenting." They knew very little in advance about eating arrangements on board; a 'tweendecks passenger would certainly have welcomed such information, but it turned out after all not to be crucial: Rosalie was invited to take meals with the captain, and she spurned her mother's advice to try to supply herself with a goat and some chickens so that she might have milk and fresh eggs at sea. "I am afraid a goat would be a somewhat troublesome traveling companion and the captain has already seen to chickens." The chickens were evidently allowed to move about freely on board, for later on Rosalie lamented that they had eaten up her precious flowers, a fuchsia and a heliotrope.

"The bosun has been kind and promised to help me stow my things. I am quite fond of him although it strikes me as somewhat awkward to have a young baron in attendance, but the two passengers between decks look too exalted for me, so I think I shall be content with him in the long run. I should very much like to have some striped shirting as a curtain around my wash stand. The captain has said that if there is anything I desire I need only let him know and I shall have it if at all possible. This morning the bosun came with coffee before I had had time to finish dressing, and I crept back into my bunk and latched the door. The first thing I intend to ask of the captain is a hook and eye so that I can lock up from inside. The only one of the hands I have become acquainted with is the quartermaster; he is from Gevle, his name is Elfstrand. I like him too; he has promised to teach me sea terminology."

Sandhamn, 20 August: "Daddy, you will perhaps enjoy hearing how I have spent my days since I last wrote. I have been in good health and in fairly good spirits and have been ashore every day. Holmström the customs inspector has a fortepiano; he is musical and was thrilled when on Sunday I played duets with his daughters; he declared that Captain Valley was welcome to stay here another three months. He wanted me to come ashore at eight the following morning and play with them! . . . It remains to be seen when the wind will come up and we can be on our way. It was all to the good that we were delayed here a few days since in that time I have been able to get myself settled."

21 August: "We cannot sail because of stiff headwinds. God keep it from lasting too long, for although I do find it quite pleasant here, it will seriously delay our arrival. The captain makes out that he always has had such bad luck whenever he has taken passengers aboard that he has just about decided never to accept such cargo again. . . .

"Nothing has been said so far about special arrangements for my coffee, nor do I think there will be. When the bosun comes up at seven with the captain's coffee, he invites me at the same time and then I am dressed and waiting, for I have absolutely no inclination to let him peek into my quarters. I now have had a hook installed on the door so that I can latch it from inside."

Sandhamn, 21 August: "It would be dreadful to be down there between decks. The big woman, the one Mama spoke with, is a housekeeper named Bina who intends to make her way in the world, win or lose. She is said to have the same unfortunate tastes as Christine, so that the captain has been requested not to let her go ashore. The other one is a spinster from Norrköping on her way to a relative in Mobile. They get ship's fare entirely, except for tea in the evening instead of peas which are served at every noon meal and every evening. . . . I have as yet not used anything but a little crisp bread from my stock, for the ship's rusks are quite hard; so I plan to make up a little toddy sometimes in order to get away from the daily diet of peas, but we are still getting milk from ashore; we have also had raspberries."

Helsingör Road, 1 September: "A long interval, Mutter dear, nor did I suppose I would be continuing this evening. . . .Oh what days I have been through since I last chatted with you, Mama! As far as physical suffering is concerned, the worst I have experienced, and I never thought I would get back enough strength to be able to hold a pen. In fact the other night I thought my last hour was at hand, but felt no fear, however, just wished that it soon would be over, for the torment I experienced when my head first was twisted straight down then suddenly upward was truly torture; I was so sick then, too, and weak.

"There was not a moment's rest the entire night, the ship was practically under water, one mammoth wave after the other washed over the deck and even penetrated into the cabin; one of the yards, thick as a maypole at the lower end, broke in half, also the iron fittings, and I was tossed about in my bunk like a little mitten. I had almost, or to say the truth had definitely, decided to return home from Helsingör, for I did not believe it would be possible to arrive whole in Charleston. I was afraid, however, that father would not like it, and since I am now so much better that I can get about on my own, it is just as well that I finish what I have begun. Whether I will ever have the courage to return—that will be another story. . . .

"However, I have now arranged for Mlle. Marie (not the former housekeeper . . . but the woman from Norrköping, who has advanced quite suddenly to being called "Mamsell" though she had previously been the personal maid of a Miss Nordenstolpe with whom she had been ever since she was eleven years old) to help me out a little when I am in a complete muddle. She is very kind and helpful . . . and was a real find, for it was too difficult to be without a woman's support in such a state of helplessness. Besides, she has an excellent trait: she is never seasick. The captain is very considerate and friendly toward me; when the weather has been such that I have not been able to be up and about, my mattress has been carried up on deck where I have lain with his huge raincoat spread over me. . . .

"4 p.m. What treasures, more precious than those of Peru or of California, that the captain handed me today when he came aboard! Letters, letters from home, and what letters, so good, so loving! They could raise the dead and they even woke up the half-dead. I read—no, I rather flew through them, for I was to go ashore with the captain; I danced, I wept, I laughed, I was happy again, I think life has perhaps been restored!"

The ship remained at Helsingör for four days for repairs and provisioning. In that time Rosalie wrote home of excursions she and others had taken into the Danish countryside and of the new friends she was making aboard ship. On the way through the Kattegat Rosalie wrote, 5 September 1851, to her brother Emil, the naval cadet: "I have not yet felt any regrets or anxiety over the steps I have taken though often missing my home and the dear ones I have left behind. I feel now, thank God, calmness within my own breast; the storms have played out there, and all is well. If only I am equal to the tasks that lie ahead and have strength enough to work for my own existence! I believe however that these exertions will be of benefit to me, that the necessity of providing for myself will sharpen my wits and keep my thoughts from ceaselessly ranging over the unhappy subjects that lie so close at hand." From the North Sea she wrote a few days later to her father: "Hopeful of sending greetings from the Channel to all my dear ones at home, I have spent some time each day in writing when weather and wind have permitted. We could not have wished for lovelier weather than we have had every day, almost without a break, since our departure from Helsingör, although no doubt the sailors would have wished to have a somewhat stiffer breeze. All the same, it seems to me we have made good progress since we now begin to glimpse Old England, and high in the rigging where the captain has taken his place it is said that they can make out both towns and churches. The picture begins now to become more exciting! large sailing vessels, a good many Dutch, English, and French fishing boats, as well as several steamships. . . . The captain and I occasionally speak English to each other; he is fairly well at home in it. He has been at sea for 26 years and has sailed mostly to America, visited New York more than twenty times. He is, however, no friend of that country, or rather its people, claiming that there is more despotism there than in most of the monarchies of Europe, since in the elections people in subordinate positions are absolutely obliged to obey the wishes of their superiors and the victorious party fills all posts with their own people, dismissing the others no matter how well qualified and capable they may be."

The pilot came aboard and all letters were given into his care. Rosalie tried speaking English with him but found it difficult to understand him since he "spoke too fast." When the tide was not in their favor in the Channel and the wind was light, they had to lower anchor so as not to be driven back. Now it was no longer possible to send letters home, and the sea diary takes over the narrative. The usually troublesome voyage past the Bay of Biscay proceeded smoothly in weather so fine that the captain claimed he had never seen its like.

14 September 1851: "We came upon a large American frigate, which steered hard aport. Its name was 'Fanny' out of Baltimore; it probably carried emigrants since the decks were crowded with people. Supposing that we were countrymen of theirs, they spread out their flag over the side, and we in turn showed the Swedish flag but without either flag being run up; both sides remained too stubborn. The American, with many sails on the lee, sailed by us, but that was not to Captain Valley's liking, and a lee sail was added on here and we soon caught up with her although she was now on our starboard side. The American also seemed to have a hanker-

ing for a race, for we saw some of their people busy hoisting a topsail. This sailing match continued a little longer, but after a while there was too much distance between us since they sailed a more northerly route."

Rosalie gave serious thought during the month-long crossing to the natural forces that assaulted the ship from time to time and was pleased to be able to record in her diary that she had not given way to fear even in the worst storms and the heaviest seas. She passed the time keeping herself and her gear in good order, occasionally sewing and reading. She regularly enjoyed pleasant though wary conversations with the captain, who was rabid on the subject of American egotism and deceitfulness. The days grew warmer, and before long all hands had turned to, scrubbing and rinsing and polishing in preparation for making port at Charleston.

20 October 1851: "Up early to watch the sunrise, which in truth was magnificent, but how to find words for what is indescribable! The captain was in high spirits since the voyage had gone so well; he had been up all night and taken soundings every hour; we also had a steady wind so that he hoped that by midday we might catch sight of Charleston. The soundings continued; the first time I came up on deck they were thirteen, later eight fathoms, at which point it remained. Large numbers of seagulls swooped around us. Around nine o'clock the captain went up to the topgallant crosstrees and saw land and the lighthouse at Charleston. Activity on board grew livelier still, and even I wanted to take part in all that was going on but could do nothing other than help the bosun run up the pennon. Around ten o'clock I could discern with the naked eye a long dark strip on the horizon—that was America; a bright tower—the lighthouse at Charleston. I felt utterly downhearted. What fate would I, poor lonely child, encounter in this foreign land? Oh, I felt more like a child now than ever! I felt need of a warm loving heart to lean on, a strong hand to support me, but I looked for them in vain. . . . I had to go below to the cuddy to weep and pray; then I felt better.

"Several large steamboats were to be seen. At eleven o'clock a pilot came aboard, one of whose rowers was a Negro. . . . The pilot had brought with him a newspaper, the Charleston 'Evening News,' which I studied and to my surprise found in it a story, 'The Right One,' by Fredrika Bremer; I had read it in 'Nordstjernan.'[3] . . . Around three o'clock we had got up to 'the bar' outside Charleston just at high tide; otherwise we would have had to lower anchor, for the water at ebb tide is only two fathoms deep in the most shallow places. At four thirty I see the city quite

3 *The North Star*, an annual which in 1844 had been devoted exclusively to Fredrika Bremer's fiction.

well, and we sail by the lighthouse situated on the outermost island to the left of the entrance to the harbor. Then, James and John's Islands. A great many butterflies flutter around us, yellowish brown, almost the same color as velvet roses, and with black spots. On the right is Sullivan's Island with many small houses, each one with piazzas and embedded in greenery. It all looks very attractive.

"We arrived too late to go ashore in the evening and lowered anchor a short distance from the city. A Swedish vessel, the brig 'Elise,' in which Captain V. had a share, lay in the road. It saluted us with the Swedish flag and after a while several gentlemen came aboard. . . . I left the gentlemen in undisputed possession of the cuddy, where they drank, smoked, and talked while I sat curled up on the taffrail to which Mlle. Bina had accompanied me giving me an account of her past fortunes. Boats came up alongside the vessl and the rowers asked if we wanted to go ashore, but I did not care to. Finally the cuddy became unoccupied, and the gentlemen went off in the company of the captain. I went below and had my evening meal consisting of the last of the lingonberries and the last pepparkakor,[4] then crept into my bunk."

21 October 1851: "Up early in the morning to get my things and myself in order. Not so easily done, since there was scrubbing and scouring going on everywhere, and it was only with difficulty that I could get dressed, for the skylight had been pushed partly to one side and the sailors were right over my head; I got through this unpleasantness, however, by reminding myself how soon I would be away from it."

---

4 Cookies not unlike ginger snaps but thinner and usually flavored with cardamom as well as other spices.

III

ARRIVAL AT CHARLESTON; ON TO LIMESTONE

Rosalie wrote to her mother from Charleston, 25 October 1851: "Mr. [Hjalmar] Hammarsköld came down to the ship on Tuesday morning to fetch me and brought a carriage with him so that the lady might ride, God bless us! A Mr. [Niklas] Bahr had come along also, Swedish and some sort of shipping agent here. I who was not ready to go ashore so soon since I thought the customs officers would first come aboard now hurriedly threw on some clothes, packed a few things while the gentlemen waited. Mr. Hammarsköld had received letters from Cooperville, so that he was prepared for my arrival, and as soon as he had a report that I had come, he went and got a carriage to fetch me without first going home, so that when we reached here no one was expecting us, and Mrs. Emilie Hammarsköld was taken quite by surprise but received me with the greatest friendliness and so also did her mother, an old granny—well, granny is not really what she is, for she is of precisely the same age as my own little Mutter.

"I felt as though I were in a dream, like a princess in 'A Thousand and One Nights,' for that is just about how I was treated, and wherever my eyes turned they came upon new, unusual, remarkable objects. We rode from the dock in a splendid, elegant carriage driven by a Negro, traveled through broad streets with trees on both sides, between houses most of which are built in a style unfamiliar to me. There I saw weeping willows, oleanders covered with flowers, trees whose names I did not know, small gardens with camellias, several kinds of roses, and on the streets crowds of all gradations from so-called black to white. Everywhere, bustle and animation; everywhere, something new to see.

"It is a little paradise here at the Hammarskölds'. They live in a quite small house which they recently purchased with a garden attached. Along the length of the building extends a piazza furnished with green jalousies, sofa, chairs, a ceiling lamp; climbing plants grow along the exterior. Doors lead into the parlor, what we would call the 'förmak,' the prettiest of the rooms though small, nearly or not quite as large as ours, with no fewer than six windows, the lower half of each of which is hung inside the upper half so that it can be raised, green shutters, which are closed on the outside to keep out the heat. The furniture consists of small sofas, rocking chairs, and other chairs covered in black horsehair, a superb Rosenvall grand piano, a small escritoire or, as it is called here, a whatnot, since on it are placed books, flowers, and odds and ends, or it is used as a writing table, sewing table, etc. In addition, two other tables, on which are bell glasses placed over birds gleaming in the most gorgeous colors, stuffed of course. There are also stuffed birds, shells, and divers curiosities on the fireplace mantel. On the wall are hung portraits of the King, the Queen, and Jenny Lind. Adjacent there is a dining room with a pantry, and in the former there are stairs up to the bedroom and to Grandmother's two small rooms, where your Rosa finds herself for the time being. (It is not a very good place for writing, for I am often interrupted, partly by Grandmother, who comes and chats with me, partly by the little children. There are three of them here: Emily 6 years old, Coralli 4, and Edvard 2.) I say 'Du' to Mrs. Hammarsköld; I say 'Tant' to her mother Mrs. Holmberg, and I am not looked on as a stranger here but they have been so kind and have invited me to stay with them until next week when in company with Mr. and Mrs. Hammarsköld I shall travel to Columbia and from there to Cooperville."

Rosalie's sea diary continues the description of her new circumstances in Charleston: "In the evening some Italians came who were to give a concert the next day. There was music making the whole evening, which delighted me not a little. Between times we took refreshments in the form of apples, bananas, conserves, and wine. When the guests had departed and we had talked a while about our dear homeland, I went upstairs with Mrs. Holmberg where a bed had been made ready for me in her outer room, but it did not have a frame for mosquito netting. The regular beds are very large, a bed for one person being larger than our double beds, with a support between the bedposts over which is hung a net of gauzy nettle cloth to keep out the mosquitoes. Since the season for them is almost past, however, I was not particularly troubled."

Again from the sea diary, 22 October 1851: "In the morning Emilie and I went out to several stores. King Street is the principal shopping street. It is not broad, and on both sides the sidewalks are covered with awnings to protect the pedestrians from the intense heat. The stores are remarkably pretty and elegant, so deep they look like salons. Often there are mirrors fitted into the wall opposite the entrance so that you can't see the farther end. In the evenings when they are illuminated by gas, they are especially beautiful. We went into an apothecary which looked like an elegant tea room, where we drank lemonade gazeuse blended with pineapple extract. Also into a fruit store where all sorts of tempting fruits stimulated the appetite: grapes, pineapples, bananas (long, yellow, almost like thick cucumbers, but more rounded at the ends; when the skin is removed the meat is excellent, sweet, mealy, with a taste that cannot be described). In addition, oranges, pomegranates, figs, tamarind pods, dates, walnuts, and several kinds of nuts the names of which I have forgotten. Emilie bought dates and nuts and also a small jar of guava jelly made from a fruit grown in one of the West Indies.

"When we came home, I went with [J. G.] Aspelin (recently arrived from Sweden and acting for the time being as a clerk for Hammarsköld) down to the dock in order to bring my things ashore. I did not have long to wait . . . and the trunk together with Hahr's box were loaded into the boat and no customs spy put his hand on them, so that that fear of mine came to an end. During the night five of the crew had jumped ship.

"Later that evening we went to a concert in the Hibernian Hall. This hall is rather handsome, though not large, and the audience was small. The singing was quite good, and I was greatly moved. Emilie played 'The Last Rose of Summer,' an Irish ballad set by Herz. She is very sweet and I heard a voice behind me say, 'Mrs. Hammarsköld, she is so <u>sweet</u>.' There we also ran into Gomoglio, an Italian who had been at the Hammarskölds' the previous evening and had said that he was a refugee from Milan because of his political beliefs. I was greatly amused by his ideas about Sweden, of which he had particularly vague notions that I tried to correct a little."

The sea diary, 23 October 1851: "In the morning I wrote home a little, unpacked and put things away, in the course of which I had some fairly trying assistants, namely the children, who vied with one another in dragging my things around. I had a little crisp bread and rusks left which I gave to Mrs. Hammarsköld. She was altogether delighted with my rye rusks and said she would give a great deal to be able to obtain some." In her letter of 25 October to her mother Rosalie had written admiringly of her hostess's ability to assist in the household economy: "Emilie is a very accomplished pianist and her talents have contributed very considerably to their present state of affairs. In addition to her post as organist, which brings in $400 a year, she gives lessons daily at $1 an hour and also assists at concerts."

The sea diary, 24 October 1851: "In the morning out in the garden and picked roses and violets; wrote, played the piano, talked. In the evening to the theater and saw a French company in a ballet. The theater was small and ugly; on the first row le beau monde could be seen in elegant toilets, and many beautiful faces, but not many people were there. Charlestonians are very religious and those who are 'members of the church,' that is to say, belong to a congregation, are not allowed to go to plays and balls. The ballet was rather mediocre." Rosalie continued in the letter of 25 October to her mother: "A pantomime was performed which was too slapstick to be amusing. Best of all I liked the polka performed by a M. and Mme. Montplaisir with great liveliness, boldness, and abandon, just as it should be in a country dance; the ending was truly wild and the storm of applause was also wild. Never have I heard such din in a theater: clapping of hands, stamping of feet, pounding with canes, shouts, all to express approval.—From the theater we went to Rutjes' Confectionery, where a long room furnished with small marble tables along the walls is set aside within the store for ladies when they wish to take some refreshment. We said therefore that this time the gentlemen were in the shelter of our wings. We had a fine little supé and then went home."

25 October 1851: "In the morning I went with Grandmother to the Market, which is Charleston's version of a market square. It is a very long building with a walkway down the middle and tables on both sides for the sellers. It is divided into several departments and every fresh foodstuff needed or desired can be found there: beef, veal, lamb, and pork, venison, poultry both alive and killed, all kinds of vegetables, fruits, fish, etc. It was truly great fun to take this promenade and to see the crowds of people there. In the afternoon we took a tour outside the city by carriage; when the streets came to an end (they are, however, not cobbled) we rode in the country on a road made of logs for the dust would otherwise have been choking. We drove very fast and I did not see much more than that the land is flat and the vegetation luxuriant. Vines run between the trees, among which the live oak was especially beautiful with long white moss hanging from the branches. . . . It is so warm here that during the first days I could not endure having as much on me as at home at the height of summer, only a chemise, a couple of petticoats, and a muslin dress, yet I was hot through and through. During the final weeks at sea I had no more on than that, although of course I had worn a cotton dress instead, and in that fashion I sat up all day long and did my work. Poor me, if I had taken Axel's advice never to go out on deck without a coat and knitted bonnet or hood, I would surely have disappeared in a cloud of steam. . . .

"Scarlet runner beans, spinach, peas, radishes, and turnips have just been sown here, since they grow during the winter months. Roses are still in bloom: the same day I came, I received of Mr. Hammarsköld a remarkably beautiful dark red rose taken from a bush on which thirty different kinds had been grafted. I had as a corsage to wear to the performance one of the most beautiful of the China roses and two white rosebuds which I had picked out in the garden. Sweet violets grow here abundantly; I shall send a couple home. Canna indica grows shoulder high like a weed, also convolvulus and verbena. Emilie came and gave me a couple of ripe figs which she had gathered today. . . .

"The Negroes are not gleaming black, but brown-skinned, looking as though they were covered with soot; their lips also are almost black, very thick, the hair just like wool. The headdress of the women consists of a picturesquely arranged cotton neckerchief; in other respects they dress like the whites though not so elegantly. Here [at the Hammarskölds'] there are three Negroes, two women and one little boy; one of the former is their own, the other two have been hired from their owner."

From the sea diary, 26 October 1851: "We were in the church [St. Peter's] where Emilie plays. It is on Logan Street opposite the Hammarskölds' house. It is Episcopal and it is extremely beautiful. The service closely resembles that of the Lutheran church but the congregation gets down on its knees for prayers. There is no altarpiece; toward the back of the church there was a platform, decorated with a red cloth, which was used as a pulpit. Below it was a kind of bench where the priest officiated from time to time. The congregation has a priest whose pay is 1200 [dollars] (not much in Charleston) and he has to preach three times every Sunday in addition to a sermon every Tuesday, marry, baptize, bury, visit and comfort the sick, and most difficult of all, keep a watchful eye on every member of the congregation since the priests are thought to bear the responsibility for their souls. The singing is not slow and solemn as ours is. There were fans and palm leaves lying all about in the pews. In the middle of the service there was a loud crash as though a bomb had exploded in the vicinity, and the church shook as jagged bolts of lightning crossed back and forth in the sky. It was a little sample of thunder in the South.

"Some of the Swedes came in the afternoon 'to look at our little rose,' Hammarsköld said. Besides Aspelin they were Myhrman, whose father is a department head in [the Swedish] government and who arrived at Charleston after me; Schultze; Tengberg from Lidköping, whom we call Magister; and finally Wessman. After we had talked for a while, we took 'supper' at 6:30 and then sat down to a [card] game of 'kille,'—N.B.: after the shutters had been securely fastened, since an American would have regarded this as an atrocious sin." In a later letter to her mother, 6 November 1851, Rosalie remembered how the Swedes ate up the last of the crisp bread with great delight that day and added: "Sundays here are held to be very holy; church services are never to be neglected; no pastime or work is to disturb the day of rest. If Americans could see how the sabbath is employed in Sweden, they certainly would suppose us to be no less than pagans."

The sea diary, 28 October 1851: "The train was to depart for Columbia at 8 in the morning, and we started out early to be on time at the station, where we met fellow countrymen and Wessman, who brought with him a parcel of oranges and pomegranates." Rosalie remembered later to give her father details of the train journey in a letter dated 9 November 1851: "The road to Columbia, the capital of South Carolina, is a distance of 130 miles and was covered in little more than eight hours, although I think the train stopped thirty times for passengers to get on and off, to take on wood and water; anyway, this railroad, which is the oldest in America, is said never to go very fast.[1] It is quite pleasant riding on a steam train; in the beginning I felt a bit ill, but that soon passed. In the car in which we rode there was room for 62 persons not counting the so-called ladies' saloon located at the rear and set aside exclusively for ladies. We sat on small sofas covered in red shag, each seating two persons with a little armrest between them and a backrest which could be shifted front or back at will. These small sofas were placed on both sides of the car which was furnished with windows that could be raised and lowered and with green blinds, and in the middle was an aisle. There was also a little iron stove.

"We enjoyed the journey very much. Mrs. Hammarsköld is a well-educated and much travelled woman; she has been in Germany, Belgium, and France and besides has travelled about in America, having given concerts when she first arrived here, and so is interesting to talk to."

The sea diary picks up the narrative again: "On the way we saw the Italians again, and around 4 we arrived at Columbia covered with soot and smoke so that the first thing we had to do when we got to the American Hotel was to perform our ablutions on a grand scale. Afterwards we went down to supper, and then Hammarsköld asked if we would like to see a troupe of so-called Ethiopian singers who were giving a performance in the hotel. Emilie was tired, but I went down and this too was new to me. In a large room lighted by a small lamp and five or six candles a platform had been set up at one end and the remainder was taken up by

---

1 After the explosion in 1831 of "The Best Friend," the first steam engine to be built in America for use on a railroad, the rules on the Charleston & Hamburg line were revised to limit the speed of single-car trains to 15 mph and of multiple-car trains to 10 or 12 mph. Other lines practiced similar caution although not excessive speed but the mistake of tying down the safety valve on the boiler had caused "The Best Friend" to explode.

benches for the audience. The troupe consisted of white men dressed up as Negroes and imitating their speech, mannerisms, dancing, and jokes in the most absurd way. My pen is too feeble to give you a description of it, but I am sending you the program."

There was little time to see much more of Columbia before Rosalie had to start on the next leg of the journey by train to Chester. She wrote to her mother 6 November 1851: "On Friday morning I left Columbia, a newly laid out city which in time will surely be very beautiful, for it is well situated and has especially broad streets planted with three to four rows of trees." As she was to explain to her father, 9 November 1851, last minute changes had brought momentary confusion: "I received a letter from Hulda Thursday evening saying that she could not get away but that her brother Franz would be able to meet me Friday at Chester so that I could reach Limestone on Saturday, for it would not do to travel on Sunday. This took me aback somewhat, for Mr. and Mrs. Hammarsköld had promised to accompany me to Chester on Saturday. He and Mr. Aspelin, however, came with me as far as Winsborough [Winnsboro], where he had some errands. When they said goodbye to me I felt myself for the first time to be quite alone and abandoned in this foreign country, but it was not too dreadful, for Hammarsköld had asked the conductor to look after me, and at the station a little past Chester I was met by a gentleman (in America there are only gentlemen!) who had driven Hahr to Chester and was to bring us both back to Limestone.

"I traveled to Chester in a diligence and there made the acquaintance of Franz Hahr, who in appearance rather resembles Hulda though much fatter, but he is evidently not so fortunate as to have her cheerful, happy disposition. . . .

"About 2:30 we left Chester, where we had eaten dinner, and we now had to be content with a less speedy mode of transportation than I had been used to. We proceeded no faster than step by step, for the roads were so wretched beyond all description that Bronäsvägen and Bjurums allé when at their worst would seem magnificent in comparison with these." Not unwilling to let her family know what trials her courage had been put to, Rosalie continued her description of the journey to Limestone in a letter of 6 November to her mother: "Fairly often there were hills like Hästbräckan and much worse, but worst of all was fording Broad River, a river wider than Göta älv and with many strong currents down into which we had to go. The water gushed high over the wheel hubs, and we had to shift direction many times in order to avoid the currents. Moreover, the water was so muddy that we could not see the river bottom but had to take our chances. What do you say to that? I do not think that any power in the world could have persuaded you, Mama dear, to travel across it. It also seemed to me as though this river would separate me forever from the rest of the world. The year before, it had once risen so much that it was twenty-seven feet higher than now, and several buildings standing a distance away had then been under water. And a short time ago a whole family together with horses and Negroes drowned while trying to cross. Around 7 in the evening we arrived at our quarters for the night, a plantation twelve miles from Chester."

Rosalie left behind a description of neither the plantation nor the last day of travel over some forty miles of wretched roads. It must have been with immense relief that she finally reached her destination when the carriage rolled up late in the afternoon in front of Limestone Springs Female High School, there to be welcomed by Hulda Hahr and led between rows of curious schoolgirls to the room she would share with Hulda.

Limestone Springs Female High School had been founded in 1845 by two Englishmen, Dr. Thomas Curtis and his son William, both Baptist ministers and most recently employed as teachers, the father in Charleston, the son in Columbia. Dr. Curtis had emigrated in 1833 from England with his children as a recent widower. He had studied at Oxford, where he had made a reputation for himself in theology, and he had taken a lively interest in the school reforms which had received their impetus in Europe after the French Revolution. Dr. Curtis had investigated school conditions, especially in France, and had become convinced of the merit of the growing demand for better education for girls in order to make of them better mothers.

After more than ten years' experience in schools in both the northern and the southern states, Dr. Curtis had had the good fortune to acquire at a very reasonable price a large hotel only ten years old to which were attached an extensive park and gardens. The site was regarded as being particularly salubrious, and the hotel had been established in connection with mineral springs intended to become a popular retreat in the summer months from the heat of the Low Country of South Carolina and Georgia.[2] Several persons had built homes there, among them former Governor

---

2 Limestone Springs had been established on 900 acres, mostly woodland, in the mountains of South Carolina at the height of the vogue in America for mineral springs as a therapy against all manner of ailments. Its organizers hoped especially to stimulate land and housing speculation in the area by attracting wealthy planters and their families from the coastal regions of Georgia and South Carolina seeking relief from the summer heat of the Low Country and from "country fever" caused, as it was thought, by the "miasma" rising from the ground during hot summer nights. The hotel, a four-story brick structure 274 feet

David Johnson of South Carolina, who took a warm interest in the school. He appears in Rosalie's letters home.

Given the bad roads, it is scarcely surprising that the hotel soon fell on hard times. But the school survived despite such difficulties and continues today as Limestone College. Over the years new buildings have been added to the original hotel, which serves still as the nucleus of the entire establishment. In the school catalogue for 1849 mottoes are printed on the first page: "We daily forget how soon and how much the boys and girls, now at school, will become the bad or good men and women of the next generation" (Watts) and "The true perfection of discipline in a school, is the *maximum* of watchfulness with the *minimum* of punishment" (Coleridge). These were progressive objectives for their time when learning was still being drummed into the members of the male sex and girls generally had to content themselves with cultivating their talents for household economy. It was announced also that the school was "strictly literary and in no respect sectarian." Moreover, the emphasis would be placed on having the students think, not merely memorize. Much weight was given in the curriculum to English, American history, geography, and mathematics, but the classical languages and French were also taught. A special fee was levied for lessons in French and drawing since these were extra subjects taken as electives. There were no classes on Saturdays, when the morning hours were to be spent in sewing.

The school year, divided into two terms, lasted from the middle of February until the middle of December in order to minimize the problems

---

long and 40 feet wide, was begun in 1835 and completed five years later at a cost of $75,000; there were also numerous wooden outbuildings and facilities for horse racing. When the project defaulted, Thomas Curtis bought the property for $10,000 from the state bank holding the mortgage and in 1845 founded the Female High School, the first institution in South Carolina for the higher education of women. As Rosalie reports in her letters, Curtis had to contend with bad roads that no doubt had been largely accountable for the failure of the resort, but in a few years' time a railroad line was laid within fifteen miles of the school.

The school emphasized in its catalogues the healthfulness of its location and the "careful" instruction that "the young ladies" received in a variety of subjects—"everything that is common to the principal sects of the country." "It is called a Female High School, from the effort to offer every branch of a superior American education to the pupils." And because the convenient location required no serious "estrangement from home" or disruption of "family guidance," it was "in all respects a SOUTHERN SCHOOL." *Catalogue of the Instructors and Pupils in the Limestone Springs Female High School* (Columbia, S.C., 1859), pp. 17, 18, 22, 23. Limestone Springs later became the center of Up Country debate on secession, and Dr. Curtis was a representative to the South Carolina convention voting in favor of secession. In 1860 he fired all teachers from the North rather than "allow them to pervert the minds of his Southern students." Moss, p. 207.

brought on by the possible scarcity in winter of both fuel and food. In season, the large garden supplied the school with quantities of vegetables. Mrs. William Curtis clearly did not have an easy task of managing the large household—in 1851 there were about 90 pupils and 12 teachers—and of instructing the girls in domestic and social duties. Examinations were held in July, when a group of distinguished gentlemen would be invited to listen to and also to take part themselves in the interrogations which continued for a couple of days. Then they were requested to pass judgment on the results. On one such occasion it was said that among other things "Dr. Curtis's pupils have in a particularly convincing way refuted the old superstition that women are not capable of acquiring as much knowledge as do men."

Rosalie soon discovered that her friend Hulda's optimistic letter to her about a position in the school was not grounded in any realistic assessment of the facts. For one thing, the school year was drawing to a close; for another, the need for teachers in French, drawing, and music, the only subjects Rosalie could have considered teaching until she had become more proficient in English, had been fully satisfied. The Curtises received her hospitably, however, and she was invited to put up at the school until the end of the term.

She wrote to her brother-in-law 5 November 1851: "You are perhaps wondering how things are going for me here, but it is as yet not so easy to say. However, they are far better than I had dared hope, for as you know, I was almost terrified of Americans, but so far at least I have been shown nothing but kindness and consideration. I am particularly fond of one of the teachers, Miss Tooker. She must be about twenty-two, is very good-looking, and teaches English grammar, Philosophy, Arithmetic, and Writing. She brings her work and visits with me in her free periods, when we converse to the best of my ability, but I assure you, it is just about all I can do both to understand and to speak, so that I am often painfully aware of seeming stupid. All the same, I had the pleasure of hearing from Hulda as well as from the other teachers that I exceeded their expectations, that I spoke fairly correctly, and that I should soon master the language. . . . I want so very much to be allowed to stay here where I have Hulda and Heddie Hammarsköld and several others I like, over against getting into some family out here in the country where they are not very cultured and where my dependence would weigh very heavily. Nor is it easy to find a vacancy for a governess since they attach so little importance to foreign languages but require all the more a meticulous study instead of their own. . . . Hulda does not yet know if a vacancy will open up for a music teacher, but should it, then God only knows if I can presume to accept it, for it is not easy when one has such competent colleagues as Hulda and her brother.

"I am going to make a vest in cornflower blue, have bought the material and silk for it, but not for the pleasure of giving it to one of my dear ones, but in order to try to sell it so that I may have some way of obtaining a little money. My journey from Charleston here was downright dear: it cost $20 to get to Chester and the 40 miles from there will surely be more than $10. I do not know yet since Hahr was my treasurer and he wants to wait with the reckoning until my trunks arrive, which I long to have here."

From letters dated 6 and 11 November: "I shall tell you how the days are scheduled. The morning bell rings at 6 in the winter, 5 in the summer. A half-hour is allowed for dressing, after which the bell rings for prayers and we all assemble in the chapel, a large, beautiful room with a sort of pulpit to the rear, several rows of benches, two fortepianos—one of them Hulda's, a little melodion. The service begins with a hymn, sung to the accompaniment of the last-named instrument. Then Dr. Curtis or his son reads a chapter from the Bible and then says an improvised prayer during which everyone kneels. Then follows practice in etiquette as all the girls advance and shake hands with the gentlemen, while we—the instructresses and I—depart sans façon. You will be interested to hear that in America one need not be as polite as at home. It is not required to curtsey and bow, and especially in the beginning it was difficult for me not to make my compliments. People come and go without a word of greeting or leavetaking, or if anything at all, they do it by shaking hands or at the most, giving a little nod; women friends kiss each other.—Breakfast is at 8, consisting of coffee, tea, fresh warm rusks and cornbread (they bake three times a day), butter (very good), and salt herring or meat, and hominy (= corn porridge). School begins at 9, stops at 12. Dinner at 1, at which are served a meat course, pork, beef, turkey or chicken with stuffing, sweet potatoes, beets, and rice, also wheat rusks and cornbread, sometimes a pudding or a pie, but seldom soup, which is very little used in America. Nor are there napkins. School begins again at 3, stops at 5; the supper bell rings at 6, the usual time for supper in this part of the world, when we get coffee or tea, whichever is desired, wheatbread and cornbread, butter, then pancakes or ginger snaps. The food is very good and plentiful. At 8, prayers in the chapel.

"We are called to meals at first by a big bell hung in a tree out in the yard, then by a smaller one in the hall. Then everybody hurries to the dining hall, a large room in the basement with two long tables. At one table sits the elder Curtis at the upper end, his daughter-in-law at the lower. At the middle of the table an instructress sits on either side. Mr.

William Curtis presides at the other table. When the elder Curtis has taken his seat, he pounds on the table and says a short prayer, at the conclusion of which the plates are turned right side up (they are always laid right side down) and the serving begins, the task of the instructors and instructresses. (The food has already been placed on the table.) After breakfast Mr. Curtis raps on the table and reads the girls' names from his 'report books,' which the instructresses have submitted to him and in which conduct of the previous day has been recorded. The girl whose name has been called replies, 'Correct, sir,' or 'One, sir,' 'Two, sir,' if she has received bad marks. When all that has been taken care of, they leave the table, one row at a time, and when all the pupils have gone their way, it is the turn of the teachers. We then go into the parlor, a large, beautiful room next to the chapel which is entered through two enormous doors that slide into the walls. The parlor extends the entire width of the building and has four windows at each end and between them are placed small sofas. In the middle of the room are three large tables, around which those who have work to do gather in the evenings. At 10, the last bell is rung; the girls are then to go to bed, and a Negro comes and removes their lamps, which must then remain outside the doors to their bedrooms. The morning bell doesn't ring until 6:30 on Saturdays and Sundays, when an hour is allowed to make one's toilet. The time between the preaching and Sunday School is mostly spent in dressing, since they are not permitted to do any kind of handwork, to write, other than to their parents, or to read, except in the Bible."

Rosalie wrote to her father 12 November 1851 from Limestone: "When I wrote last week to the Hammarskölds in Charleston, I asked Mrs. Hammarsköld to inform me if she should happen to hear of a good situation for me. Next week I shall begin to study diligently; until now I have been occupied with getting myself somewhat settled, for I find it necessary to be able to feel à mon aise. I have spent these last three days scrubbing, dusting, and setting things to rights, for the service here is not excessive, and since there are neither bureaus nor wardrobes I have had to obtain shelves and nails and for the rest have had to live out of my trunks. We have two rooms, one of them fairly large with two windows. The furniture consists of one large bed, five tables, four chairs, and some trunks. I have been pottering about, turning everything topsy-turvy, removing year-old spider webs, and in the end had the pleasure of making it all rather livable so that one after the other of the teachers has come up to see how 'very nice' we have arranged it here. . . .

"I shall see about sending my diary home by some ship. Then I will also say a little about politics, about the Negroes, etc. For the time being

I would only say that my deep sympathy for the Negroes has cooled off a little, for in general they are a thousand times happier than many of our servants and seem not to feel any distress over their fate. I have not yet seen any Negro looking downcast or oppressed; on the contrary.

"The relationship between the southern and the northern states is very tense; in all likelihood it will not be so very long before the storm breaks, when South Carolina will probably lead the way. There has already been talk of war this year, but this state could not stand up alone to such superior forces, and the others have not yet come to a decision. In one month's time capital amounting to 5 million dollars was withdrawn from the bank in Charleston."

Rosalie's next letter was written to her brother Emil, the naval cadet, 17 November 1851: "Sometimes I wish so cordially to have you here, especially when I see something remarkable, something that I know would also delight you. But I do not believe that I would wish that anyone in my family would come over here—God knows if they could get on here. Our ways are really quite different after all. Just imagine, there are more than 60 young girls brought together here in one place, but nothing is ever said about having a dance or playing games. They leave the cradle at an early age and adopt at once a kind of constraint in their bearing and demeanour.[3] As for their appearance, they are more pretty than ugly and the shape of their noses is decidedly better, if I may say so, than in Sweden; likewise one often sees pretty eyes. But what we would call a beautiful face is a rarity, the features being coarser, as are also their figures, which are seldom slender and lithe, but a bit lumpish. I can't think that you would find them as attractive as Swedish girls. Instead of the pleasures that young people at home enjoy in their leisure moments, the girls here have two Societies, one called Mrs. Hemans', the other Mrs. Sigourney's, named after two authoresses. They get together, have a president, a li-

---

3 A Charlestonian who was later to become Professor of History and Belles Lettres at the College of Charleston made a similar observation on his travels in the Up Country in the late 1840s. He visited Limestone Springs and also the Moravian school for girls at Salem, N.C.: "We were invited to attend an exhibition of the Female School. . . . I dare say the girls acquitted themselves well in their respective parts, but I was struck with the stiffness which characterized them all. If they had come to school to learn to be stiff, they would all have to undergo the process of unlearning on their return home; and I believe this is true of all country female schools. The girls have not the advantage of learning manners by intercourse with good society. They acquire a sort of conventional seminary manner at school and are utterly destitute of any individual character." "Memoirs of Fredrick Adolphus Porcher," ed. Samuel Gaillard Stoney, *South Carolina Historical and Genealogical Magazine* 47 (1946), 87–88.

brarian, a tiny little library, newspapers and magazines, which the members may read. They also give lectures now and then, and I would be glad to hear one of them sometime. Some of the girls here graduate, though not many. . . ."

IV

AN INTERLUDE AT LIMESTONE HOTEL

Rosalie wrote to her mother Christmas Day 1851 from Limestone Hotel: "I said that my time has been very much taken up first of all in keeping our room tidy and dusted; however, that was not so easily accomplished, and I finally had to give up all hope of succeeding, however much it pained me not to be able to have things pleasant around me. After that, there was mending and altering, for I have already been obliged to verify the words of my fellow countryman that the wear and tear on clothing here is horrible. There are nails and splinters everywhere, ready to tear apart everything in their way. Besides that, I have scarcely one dress to wear, for nothing but high necklines are worn. . . . So I must sew collars and cuffs, which are always worn; Hulda has rejected all those I brought with me as being entirely too large, for here they must not be more than 1 or at the most 1½ inches wide. I have more than enough linen and underclothes since the laundry is done every week.

"On 17 December there were examinations for the girls who are graduating, and the next day school broke up so that the activity and bustle that formerly reigned in the big building were suddenly succeeded by a gravelike silence. Principals, teachers, and pupils as well as a number of the servants have gone their way, some of them for all time, others not to return until the beginning of school—that is, in two months. Among these was Hulda, who had been invited to accompany Mrs. Curtis to Georgia and spend the holidays with her parents. I felt very much dejected in being thus abandoned by Hulda. . . . Only Miss Wilson and Miss Roos remained in the big building. We could not stay there but had to move over to the so-called hotel. You may well imagine, Mama, that the thought of living alone in a hotel and eating table d'hôte was at first a severe trial for me. It is, however, far better than I had imagined, although there are times when I feel quite lonely.

"We came here Friday evening [19 December], but I was feeling quite feeble then, had evidently taken cold, for it had been miserably cold the whole week. My hands and feet were like chunks of ice; the water froze in the water jugs which we had placed by the fireplace in the evening. I have never in all my life felt such frightful cold; sometimes I was utterly desperate, for I could neither work nor think. I went to bed without supper, for I had a high fever. Along came Tant Hammarsköld (she has been living here at the hotel with her daughter Heddie for a couple of months) with a warm drink for me, and thinking that it was too cold in my room, she herself set about making up a fire and hung a shawl over the window so that I should not have drafts blowing on me. Mama, you cannot believe how kind she is to me. She is truly a splendid woman and has endured hard trials with honor. It is a considerable difference between sitting as queen at Skultuna Works [in Sweden] and living here in a village inn, but there is never a word of complaint nor a comparison between then and now to be heard from her lips. She is good, gentle, and helpful towards all. She left with me a pair of warm, lined galoshes when I was packing at Limestone in the cold, and gave me rugs here to nail up over the holes in the wall of my room, for much worth is placed here on always having fresh air, for which reason in addition to large cracks at the windows and doors, the walls are also furnished with air intakes, where the plaster has fallen away. In the dining room several panes are missing out of the windows.

"Sunday before Christmas Captain Carl came to fetch Tant and Heddie back to North Carolina where he and his son lease an iron works about twelve miles from here. He was reluctant to take them with him, for they have only two small rooms, of which only one has a fireplace, but Tant, who wanted to spend Christmas with her family, was not to be put off. It is quite remarkable that her health tolerates these drafty rooms, for it has been uncertain for long and she seldom feels altogether well. They left on Tuesday morning and on the same day I moved into their room, which Tant had invited me to use in her absence, partly to be able to play the piano, partly because furnished as it is with her own things brought with her from Sweden, it seemed so pleasant and comfortable in comparison with the other rooms, the only furnishings of which consist of a large bed, far larger than double beds at home, so that I feared I would get lost in it, two painted wooden tables, and some chairs of the simplest kind. In this little room which with respect to furniture and comfort is the best I have seen since I came to Limestone, I feel as though I have been set down in Sweden, and I have sufficient company in my piano and books. Tant left books and her things at my disposal. They will return January 4.

"It has been not at all Christmas-like here. For Heddie I made a little slipper, for Miss Wilson a jewelry case, just to have in any event the pleasure of being able to give something on Christmas Eve. Myself I hoped for something, namely letters from home, but hoped in vain, though I was not altogether deprived, for Hulda's dear old father had written a little letter to me which had been enclosed in Hulda's, and I was at least able to hear that my family lived and enjoyed good health. There has been and still is such a shortage of eggs here that there has been no baking. I am living for the most part on coffee and tea with bread and butter. Today we had breakfast at 8:30 when I drank coffee, ate a couple of pieces of toast and a chicken wing. Dinner consisted of chicken and cooked dried peaches, and supper at 5 o'clock of a cup of coffee and toast. Thus you see that I am not gorging myself with food and drink during Christmas. Now I must stop. . . . The worst of all is to have to economize with postage."

Three days later she wrote to her father: "I am still at Limestone without knowing where I shall finally end up earning my own keep. More than once I have felt very unhappy about it, not simply because I deeply <u>wish</u> to incur no more expenses for you, Papa, and to be able to pay back what I have already incurred for this trip, but also because I am afraid that you will think me indifferent and too much concerned with my comfort as though I did not care to look seriously for a place. God knows, however, that that has not been the case, for I have drawn up not one but many plans for achieving the desired objective, pecuniary independence. . . . I have not made use of the letter of credit and do not intend to unless I possibly set up my own household in some fashion and then would require a small sum to begin with. . . . I am also diligently studying how to manage my finances and hope to make great progress in that; at home I did not think I was wasteful in any way, but I find that I have much to learn. As proof of my progress, I beg leave to say that as soon as I have finished working in the evening, I extinguish the candle and make my way about by the light of the fire in the fireplace, and since I can obtain light for my candle from there I am saving on sulphur matches. What do you say to that? Is that not a step forward? If I had brought with me a shipload of candles and matches, I would, as they say here, 'make money.' One package of four candles, far inferior to ours, costs 40 cents, and a box of matches 10 cents.

"Franz is now my only fellow countryman remaining here, but I hardly ever see him although it was said he would be taking his meals at the hotel. Since Christmas Eve when I invited him to eat Christmas porridge with me and Miss Wilson, I have only seen him once in passing. . . .

"As for the hotel, I must, however, say that it is not like our Swedish inns or hostelries except in the appearance of the rooms and furniture in the latter. It is very still and quiet here, never any question of carousing or disturbance, and now during the holidays travelers are no embarrassment either, but when they come, everyone eats table d'hôte, where the hostess serves at one end, the host at the other."

Once again from the Christmas letter to her mother: "My days pass by rather monotonously, Sundays and workdays, Christmas Eve and Christmas all alike. They do not seem long to me, however, for I have much to do and I can say with certainty that I have never been so busy during a Christmas season as during this one. By keeping constantly occupied I try to prevent my thoughts from initiating comparisons between now and then, which would not turn out to be especially to the advantage of the present. . . . But with every setting of the sun, I thank God for being nearer my goal. 'It is so short a time, so blessed an eternity.'

"But, dear Mutter, we are not to waste precious time and space in idle musings. Our era is very materialistic and so it is best that we stick to facts. America is like no other country, for what one thinks of becoming or of occupying himself with comes to nothing, and one becomes on the contrary what one least suspected. Thus, for example, a baker who came over here the same time as the Hammarskölds ended up as a carpenter, . . . and I, who had never been able to make a drawing of a tree, have quite unexpectedly become a sketcher of landscapes and have moreover been called an artist, an honor of which I had never thought to dream. This is how it came about: On Gustaf's drawing, which I had brought with me to finish, I painted a little scene of Limestone which was shown to Mr. Curtis. It pleased him extremely and after some days he asked me if I would draw for him a view of Limestone from a small daguerreotype of the place. The picture was to be a pendant to another of about the same size as the Thersner views,[1] and the drawing was to be done on marble paper. This is a kind of thin paper brushed with glue on which crushed marble is strewn so that it is completely snow white but coarse. The drawing is made with black chalk, sponge, eraser, buckskin, cork, and a knife, and is work which makes it difficult to keep hands and clothes clean.

"Well, I replied that I neither was a landscape painter nor had attempted drawing of this kind, but I wanted to try. I then drew with Miss Wilson's guidance a small landscape from the daguerreotype, but larger than it. Mr. Curtis was especially delighted with it, and I now proceeded to my larger work, but since the daguerreotype was very indistinct, I determined to take a view of the place myself and for this Franz was kind

---

1 Ulrik Thersner published in Stockholm, beginning in 1831, a series of handsome volumes containing large architectural drawings from "past and present Sweden" (*Fordna och närvarande Sverige*).

enough to help me out with advice and instruction. The beginning was like my previous work—that is, I was dissatisfied with it and thought that it would never come out right; the sky was especially difficult. I worked at my picture for two weeks, standing at the writing desk for whole days without sitting except at meal times. There was need to hurry because Mr. Curtis wished to have it finished by examination time, for he was to set out the following day and wanted to have it with him to get it lithographed. I have, however, the pleasure of hearing that my picture won general approval and that even so severe a judge as Franz liked it, which is not saying a little [see illus. 6]. To that, dear Mama, add that when I asked Mr. Curtis about my bill for board, he answered that it was more than sufficiently paid by my picture, and you can surely imagine, Mama, how happy I was to have earned my keep for the time I have been here [at the hotel] since I must still pay for myself. The charge at the Curtises would have been $10 for everything; it is higher here, the charge is the same but laundry and candles are in addition. . . .

"I have still not secured a place; it is really not as easy as might have been supposed and as Hulda believed. Hulda, Franz, and the other teachers were almost convinced that I would be offered a place at the Institute although Hulda postponed day after day saying anything to Mr. Curtis. Finally I mustered courage and did it myself, then was obliged to hear that no vacancy was available for next year since he had engaged as many as he believed would be needed. You will appreciate how that information depressed me, and it seemed to have the same effect upon Hulda and Franz. When I discussed it with him, he said that he would not wish to let me set out on my own in this foreign country but suggested to me that I stay here and he would talk with Mr. Curtis about my getting free lodging for teaching three to five of Franz's and Hulda's pupils, for which they would therefore forego their pay. But however grateful I am for this offer, I do not wish to make use of it except as may be necessary."

Continuing her letter of 28 December to her father, Rosalie wrote: "A while ago the Captain received a letter from Sandvall[2] postmarked New York; it told laconically of his adventures, his fleeing Sweden for France, where he had to sell all his valuables to pay for the voyage to New York, where he now finds himself reduced to a destitute condition, without work. His letter disturbed me to the highest degree. 'I am still safe and sound but that in fact is all,' he writes, inquiring therewith if Hammarsköld could obtain any employment for him. From all that I have heard

---

2 Johan Sandvall (1814–67), newspaperman, publisher, and editor, who left Sweden in 1851 in the wake of financial difficulties (Mrs. Laurell's note).

and seen of this country, I would not wish to advise anyone to come over who believes he is in a position to earn his bread in his homeland, for although things are tight there too, they are not so marked with bitterness as they are here. May none of my brothers hit upon the idea of seeking their fortune in America! Those who come over with a good bit of capital perhaps succeed if they are not hoaxed too quickly by the natives, but those who come with empty hands, without knowing the language, have more adversities to combat than anyone can imagine. If I were offered the largest plantation in Carolina against an agreement to stay here for the rest of my life, I would reject it; I believe it is necessary to have been born here to be able to feel happy and I could not even consider the possibility of staying. Do not think, however, that I am dissatisfied with my experience here! No, although I have already had some bitter moments and probably will have more, I would not wish it undone if for no other reason than it can be salutary to endure a few hardships, and as a school for comfort-seekers, the slothful, and the spendthrift, America is unexcelled.

"The houses are built only for warm summers, the cold seems to come always like an unwanted guest. Here in Tant's little room, made warm and cozy with blankets and rugs, the temperature could not be raised any higher than 5 degrees [Celsius] although we had had a fire all day. The blood drained out of my hands and lips because of the intense cold. In the second week of December it was on the other hand really warm, about 18 degrees; this is the most changeable weather to be imagined. . . .

"Now I must say a little about my plans and reflections. . . ." Suggestions had been made to Rosalie regarding a position as a governess, and she planned also to investigate the possibility of moving to Winnsboro to teach music, drawing, and languages. "This is how I first got that idea: a Mamsell Louise Nettelbladt, whose father had been a merchant in Stockholm, had traveled with the Hammarskölds. She was at one time to be of assistance to them and also to keep them company, but when Hammarsköld had to leave Cooperville, they no longer needed her, so that she too was paying for herself here at the hotel, supporting herself with handwork which brought in scarcely anything, however. During the year she has been in America, however, she has not learned to speak English, since she was constantly together with Swedes. Since she wants definitely to learn the language, she has now taken lodgings at a hotel in Winsborough, where she will receive room and board in return for sewing for a certain number of hours during the day. As she is close to being forty, I counted on having her as a kind of protector if I should go there. . . . If things went well for me, Louise and I would set up our own household. . . . One advantage is that the railway line goes by there." The unexpected stay at the little hotel during the winter months provided a good and surely necessary preparation for the work ahead, since the time could be devoted to Rosalie's own intensive study of the language and to the sewing that was always begging to be done.

"English may seem easy to begin with, but it is more difficult the more deeply one studies it and wishes to learn it thoroughly, partly because of its awful pronunciation, partly because of its wealth of words. Poetry is particularly difficult. I began reading Milton's 'Paradise Lost' to the teacher of English, but did not get very far along. Miss Wilson has promised that I may continue. I am now studying Brown's 'English Grammar,' the best grammar I have seen."

During this period Rosalie secured in Hedda Hammarsköld a friend for life. After Hedda returned with her daughter from spending Christmas in North Carolina, Rosalie no longer needed to feel lonely and abandoned. In a letter to her mother 26 January 1852, she wrote: "You cannot believe how kind and dear she is, and how much I have enjoyed her company. I know of no one I have so quickly taken to and with whom I sympathize so much. Sometimes I run over to see her and can lose myself there hours at a time; sometimes she comes over to me with her work. At times she reads letters or interesting things to me which she has received from friends who have traveled about in Europe and Asia. Sometimes I am asked in for coffee which she, sitting at the fireplace, prepares herself. . . . We have been invited once to have supper with Major Sims, where everyone was kind and friendly and bade us come often. The supper, which was served at 6 o'clock, consisted of coffee and tea, butter, warm wheatbread, cheese, waffles, several kinds of cakes, conserved peaches, watermelon, quince jelly. Around 8 o'clock wine, cake, candies, raisins, and almonds were passed around."

On the same day, 26 January 1852, Rosalie's father was sent a letter telling him about Mrs. Hammarsköld's husband: "The Captain has endured a great deal and lost much since he came here. The situation that he had in Cooperville was first-rate, but without his having any inkling of the reasons for it, the contract was terminated, and he has had much trouble from the company. Also from the Swedish workmen who caused him much trouble and many losses. . . . They consider themselves well situated now, and think of trying to save money to buy a plantation in Florida, where the climate is far milder and the vegetation more luxuriant, although it is said to be unhealthful in some places and unsafe because of the Seminole Indians for whom the whites—the Christians, the civilized!—

seek to provide the same fate as that which befell their brothers. I know Captain Hammarsköld only slightly, but certainly he must be an energetic, persevering man from all I have heard about him. He worked for a time in a store in Charleston. His son Carl, a nineteen-year-old with simple Nordic features, more ugly than handsome, is generally praised for his honest, unaffected character. Fourteen-year-old Heddie is a plump, good-natured girl who also shows no regret over the happiness and comfort they have lost.

"Texas and Florida are now the subject of colonists' plans, for land and cattle are supposed to be very cheap there, almost going in want of owners, so that many Americans from these states make their way there. The prairies, which lie in between, are, however, unsafe to travel across since Indians rove about there. A young Mr. Otterson, the son of a doctor here, has just arrived home from California with twenty cents in his pockets. On the way out, he and his comrades had been overtaken and robbed by Indians. On the prairies he had seen two hundred different kinds of cactus, the seed of some of which he had taken, but these too had been stolen by the Indians. There is said to be plenty of clothing and foodstuff in San Francisco. The supply of gold is evidently not so abundant now; at least that metal is more difficult to be got at by individuals, for which reason companies are formed to work the mines.

"I am still standing at the same spot with respect to my future work, unfortunately. I certainly do not wish to remain here another winter, for I suffer so much from the cold in these drafty dwellings where the wind works its way through all the walls. . . . In many respects it is a land of contrasts—les extrêmes se touchent: freedom and slaves, cold and heat, the fastest communications and the unendurably slowest, the greatest industry and total boorishness and apathy, go hand in hand. They have had snow in Charleston this winter, the first, I think, in the memory of man. Emilie wrote that it was terrible to see the snow on the new blooms of her roses and violets. The children call it the beautiful white sand. There has also been snow in New Orleans, some ten inches deep."

Rosalie wrote joyously to her father 22 February 1852 of the letters she had received from home. Her father had evidently been ill but was now on the mend. Rosalie imagined him walking in their woods and wondered how he would like to take promenades in the forests of America with her at his side. Then she returned to the inevitable subject of her finances. "If only I could once secure a place, you would no longer, with God's help, have any expenses on my account. That is my fixed determination—that so much as it may be possible, to defray my expenses in

America. It would be a satisfaction for me to know that even I, like my brothers, would be able to earn my own bread and not always have to be receiving it. But whom have I to thank for this prospect if not my own dear parents, to whom I will therefore always be indebted."

V

A YEAR AT LIMESTONE FEMALE HIGH SCHOOL

Rosalie's prospects suddenly brightened with the New Year, as she wrote to her father 26 February 1852: "I am still here at Limestone, as you will see by the postmark on my letter, but with this difference, that I have now moved over to the school, where I have been engaged for one year as an instructress in French and music at a salary of $300. This arrangement was reached quite hastily, for a week ago I had no intimation of it. Last Monday Franz appeared and said that Dr. Curtis wished to speak with me. I went to see him, we reached an agreement, and the next day I began giving lessons. I accepted the position not without a certain trepidation, for it is not so easy to teach one foreign language in yet another. I have therefore to work a great deal on my own after classroom hours. . . . My greatest fear, however, comes from the thought of the public examination which is held every summer in July and which is usually attended by several hundred persons; last year there were five hundred here. A platform is built at that time in the schoolroom, and teachers and pupils have to make their appearance on it before the eyes of the audience. Poor little me then! I said to Franz that I feared that I would become ill of anxiety, whereupon he replied, 'So much the better, Rosa, for then you will be let off all the more easily!' There is not as much demand for foreign languages as in Sweden; only French is studied and among the 70 pupils who have now arrived (they don't all come at the same time), there are only 9 studying that language. There are more music pupils, but the motivation and talent for music, as in general for the fine arts, are very slight. They will not learn with thoroughness but only for appearance' sake so that exercises and études are soon set aside, their place taken by some pieces which generally are forgotten as soon as school is over. I have five music pupils, expect more in the afternoon. May I accomplish what I have undertaken! Now, as before, Hulda is my friend in need and my mentor, good and kind.

"Spring has fully arrived, the most glorious weather you can imagine. Plowing and planting are in full swing everywhere. Easter lilies—called 'butter and eggs'[1] here—have been out for over two weeks, and I have a bouquet of them in my room. Mr. Curtis has promised to let me have a little flower bed where I plan to sow some seeds that I brought with me from Sweden. How those flowers will be precious to me!

"These past two evenings we have had a magnificent but dreadful spectacle, a forest fire a short distance from here that looked like a sea of fire up from which rose flames, sparks, and thick clouds of smoke. I thought of you, my dear Mutter, who surely would not have dared go to bed if you had been in my place. On the first night I was at a loss to know what I should do, for several wooden buildings and fences lie between the seminary and the fire, and if the fire should break out here during the night it would be disastrous, especially for us who live on the fourth floor, since all but the outer walls are of wood. There are long piazzas, also of wood, on both sides of the building. The forest fire was set as protection against a greater fire in the vicinity!? . . . You would be amazed at the wastefulness with forests here. They never give a thought to making use of a fallen tree but leave it to rot away where it has fallen. In many places they set fire to the woods when they wish to till the land and then plant it. Where the soil is very good—that is, not here—I have heard it said that they do not bother to plow, but only here and there among the burned out stumps and dead trees they sow some seeds of corn. . . .

"Yes indeed, Father dear, I keep up enough to know of Kossuth's visit to America,[2] have even read his speech in Washington, a genuine master-piece.—You wish you could move here. Alas, Papa, it is not as simple as one may often suppose. First, what an ado would such a move not create, and then to leave behind all the comforts of a civilized life in order to settle down in what is half wilderness without ever having the opportunity of enjoying beautiful art or a cultured society. Nor would the least of it be the difficulties of speaking and understanding the language, and finally to be exposed also to all the dangers of a civil war, which is evidently not so far off. No, whoever abandons his fatherland for another must have youth on his side, youth, perseverance, and strength, for many obstacles and adversities must be overcome before a peaceful, secure life can be lived on foreign shores. I scarcely think that you and Mama would like being here. . . ."

To her mother from Limestone 3 March 1852: "I can assure you,

---

1 Name given in some parts of the South to the yellow and white narcissus (Sw. *påskliljor*, literally "Easter lilies"), particularly when double—that is, without a "trumpet."

2 Lajos Kossuth addressed the United States Senate 23 December 1851 in behalf of Hungarian independence.

Mutter dear, that it is not so easy to teach in a foreign language. I sit up in the evenings usually until 11:30 to study the lessons that will be recited for me the following day. Having access to dear Franz and the English dictionary which Elving kindly let me take with me, I do manage, however. I think of him gratefully every time I use it.

"In the afternoon there is fancy work—that is, all kinds of fine handwork, and you will appreciate how much is involved in getting so many people started in the work. Hulda and I have the section on crocheting. Mr. Curtis brings home canvases, yarns, silk, strips of cloth, beads, etc., which are handed out for a cash payment, naturally. . . .

"I keep well, thank goodness, both in body and soul. Hulda claims that you would not recognize me; my cheeks have filled out and got color, and putting on weight must make me look younger because no one will believe that I am all of 28 years. . . . This experience has no doubt been of the highest benefit to me so that I may congratulate myself for having had the courage to come to this bold decision that so many no doubt called strangely reckless. . . .

"You ask if a foreigner may not dress differently—no, indeed, that would never do, everyone has to be cast in the same mold. Our round hats which would be so excellent against both the heat and the sun, we are not permitted to wear—the whole school would surely then rise up against us. They have instead a sort of large hood called a sunbonnet, horribly ugly, but in use throughout the entire United States. Sundays when we go to church—that is, to chapel, which is in the same building—we must dress in hats and mantillas, though only for the benefit of one another. They are quite elegant then, many in silk and all handsomely got up. Dressing is for that matter the only thing they are allowed to enjoy on Sundays since reading, playing, dancing, or any sort of handwork is forbidden. Some of them dress three times a day—interesting!"

Again to her mother from Limestone, 5 April 1852: "My life here is kept very busy from 5:30 in the morning until 11 at night, but I like it; I really enjoy it, and this constant hurry and exertion leave my thoughts no time to dwell on the past, but force them to be occupied only with the present moment, and when I lie down to rest I am usually so tired that I fall asleep at once and sleep like a child. . . . You know then how little time your Rosa has at her disposal; listen to what that time is to cover: mend and alter dresses, sew a few new things, study French, botanize, play the piano, write letters, and go on visits. I am kept busy running from one thing to the next. It is distressing to be forced to sew when there is so much else to be done now when it is the loveliest season of the year, when nature with its flowers, its bird song, its warm spring breezes tempts me to enjoy all this splendor. . . . A seamstress and a shoemaker would 'make money' here. Apropos of the latter, I would take particular pleasure in receiving three or four pairs of boots in satin or preferably some other strong cloth if you should have an opportunity to send them by some ship headed for Charleston. There is no shoemaker here, but most footwear comes from New York; a good grade of cloth boots costs 2 to 3 dollars. The clay is horribly destructive to shoes, and when something goes wrong with them, it is impossible to get them repaired. And so old shoes are to be seen everywhere. If you are able to send me something, I should also like to have some black edging, a roll of narrow, black silk ribbon, a few bars of good soap, an antimacassar for my sofa, and three or four boxes of ordinary writing paper, which is not to be had here. . . . A pastry cook would have no difficulty turning a profit here, for as in all schools, the girls are hungry."

Rosalie reported that measles had broken out in the school among the pupils, the teachers, and the staff. "Mrs. Curtis has spent all day every day in the sick rooms; her own four children have also been sick. Both Hulda and I are glad we have already had it. Forty people have been sick, among others the Misses Wilson and Armstrong. I have had to be with them every moment between lessons and at night I have slept in their rooms. Thank heavens, they are better now. . . .

"On Sundays we have so-called Sunday School, consisting of lessons from the Bible. Every one of the instructors and instructresses has a recitation class; we have begun with the Pentateuch, and it is hard work in the beginning since I have to learn every lesson myself. Mr. Curtis has made me a present of a quite handsome polyglot Bible and seemed very pleased with my offer to take part in the school.

"One of my pupils in French I am especially fond of; her name is <u>Eliza Peronneau</u>, and she comes from near Charleston. Not only is she pretty but also charming and very diligent and considerate; she is 16 years old.

"Easter Day [April 11]. There is no talk of an Easter recess since the Baptists, which the principals are, do not celebrate this or any other festival day or holy day. They go on working here on Good Friday as on every other day, but I took the day off, having said to Mr. Curtis that I did not wish to teach on a day that we consider as sacred as the Sabbath. He replied that he could have no objection to that, and since Hulda and Franz have the same creed and since neither did the Episcopalians wish to teach, he gave the whole school a holiday, as they call their free days."

In a letter of 15 April 1852, Rosalie replied to her father's questions about the chances of employment in America, particularly with thought of his sons. Rosalie emphasized the importance of arrangements having been carefully planned for them before they left Sweden. If they should have prospects of obtaining any reasonably suitable and remunerative job, she would gladly support their coming over: "I am convinced that their staying here for a couple of years would do them much good. But I shudder at the thought of seeing them come here, as so many do, on pure chance, for you must admit that it is not particularly heartening for a young man with an education, used to and fond of family life and good society, to be looked on at first with a certain suspicion because no one would know his antecedents, and then to endure many reverses and humiliations only to end up, perhaps, employed at hard manual labor or standing in a shop measuring out cloth or weighing groceries. And do not think that what is demanded of teachers is so little! Enough with respect to subjects which are highly regarded at home: foreign languages, music, drawing, but ever so much more with respect to their own language, with which they take great pains, and I place great value in that. As far as the more scientific subjects are concerned, I believe the instruction they receive is fairly superficial. However, they do study Philosophy, Logic, Astronomy, Botany, Mathematics, Geometry, Algebra, and Latin. My energies have been too much fragmented for me to be able to do anything thoroughly, and the consciousness of that makes me distrustful of my own abilities. I believe that if all my powers had been directed toward one end, I would have been able to go rather far; as it is, I have dabbled in <u>much</u>, but do nothing well."

She wrote to her mother 9 May 1852 of the amount of time she had had to devote to her wardrobe with the help of Hulda and Miss Wilson. Her latest creation was a dress in mauve and white made of printed calico bought for 2½ cents a yard. "For one reason or another more dresses are needed here than at home, where the same ones can be worn winter and summer. A wool dress can be as little worn here in summer as a light cotton in winter. The matter is taken to such lengths that a dark ribbon can scarcely be worn in summer when everything must be light. White dresses are very much worn. It seems more than a little odd to see old people in white and barege. White sacques, in about the same style as for gentlemen, are very fashionable at Limestone. They are short like small jackets or perhaps like night-jackets. They are, however, excellent and cool when worn with lowcut dresses and often serve to hide defects in them."

Rosalie's letter of 21 May 1852 was addressed "to all my dear ones." Her passion for collecting and drying botanical specimens, she wrote, had spread like wildfire through the school. Dr. Curtis had proposed a botanical excursion, and he promised to award "the best <u>Flora</u> in the United States" to the girl who could present the finest herbarium at the end of the school year. He himself was now spending all his free time investigating plant life. "On May 5 in the morning Mr. Curtis sent for me, saying that he planned to make an excursion to Broad River and adding that if it would amuse me to go along, it would give him pleasure. Naturally I did not say no, but was as delighted as a little child, and at 12 we packed a little extra dinner and set out. The others in the company were Eliza Peronneau and Mrs. Curtis's sister. We made our way first to so-called Gilky Mountain—more like a hill—but as the countryside in that area is so flat, it is truly surprising what an extensive view opens up when after a little difficulty you have reached the highest point. At the foot of the mountain, in the shade of walnut trees and oaks, is a fairly large store. We left the horses and carriage there and then began our promenade up the mountain. It was exactly the most beautiful time for a visit to this place, for mountain laurel, a rather tall shrub with laurellike evergreen leaves, was in full bloom. The flowers are very beautiful, white and pink with dark brown specks, the buds curly and clustered together like the flowers of the elder, but each one the size of an anemone. They were very profuse so that the bushes shone red and white, giving off a faint but agreeable fragrance.

"After we had enjoyed the view and picked as many flowers as we could carry, we continued on the way to Cooperville, where there are an iron mine, a blast furnace, and foundry, all located right beside Broad River. The breadth of this river and its turnings, its banks, now and then hills, at other times dales, clad in bright green, the dwellings scattered on both sides, reminded me vividly of Göta älv. We got out, the horses were unharnessed and tied to a tree (it never occurs to anyone here to put the horses in a stall or give them something to eat while they are waiting), and we began our stroll along the river. The vegetation was more luxuriant there. Trumpet creeper and salpiglossis (a yellow bell, brownish within) wound their tendrils around the trees, and all the way to the top of quite tall trees one could see its flowers and so too the pink honeysuckle, whose beautiful clusters shone so brightly among the green leaves. The yellow jasmine had already finished blooming. Fringe trees with their profuse white fringelike flowers also made a quite handsome effect among the trees."

In a letter to her brother Emil a few days later, 27 May 1852, Rosalie told how little the fauna had succeeded in sharing the enthusiasm she felt for the flora. "Snakes are said to swarm all over here, but so far I have been fortunate in seeing only two of these enemies of mine, and no rattlesnake. One such, seven feet ten inches long, ten inches thick and with twenty-seven rattles, is said to have been killed not so long ago in North Carolina. A kind of insect here has bothered me very much, so-called ticks, which seem to be related to *fästingen* in Sweden and are as large as a small lady-bird. They are a nuisance, biting so hard that they have to be plucked away since their bite leaves a swelling. After a walk in the woods, you can be sure of having the pleasure of their company."

Continuing her letter of 21 May to "all my dear ones," Rosalie wrote: "We strolled undaunted among the thickets, dry leaves and twigs, but were fortunate enough not to encounter any of the creeping species other than a mocassin, a snake nearly three feet long and as thick as my arm at the wrist. We also came upon a dead cow and a dead turtle. Finally, carrying great loads of flowers, we had to think of returning and got back to the carriage tired and thirsty.

"It was not before eight o'clock in the evening that we returned after having driven quite fast over the extraordinarily bumpy, uneven road, which would surely have elicited from you, dear Mama, more than one 'oy!' On the way home, we traveled past a plantation belonging to a Mr. Graffner, which when he came there fifty years ago was only a wild pathless forest. A horrid tale is told about his wife, that she once beat a Negro woman to death and to hide the deed set fire to the cabin where the victim lived. The law is strict, however, for those who treat their slaves badly, and not long ago a person was banished for this reason from the state where he lived.

"Every state has its own laws. When Captain Hammarsköld was here a little while ago, he told how people in North Carolina had assembled in a great crowd to drive out of the state a person of bad repute, and when he could not be found, a reward had been posted for whoever delivered him dead or alive to the court. In that same region a person had been sentenced to a caning of twenty-two strokes (somewhat like the dreadful flogging in Sweden) because he had stolen a pen knife worth ten cents. Hammarsköld had witnessed punishment of that kind where the culprit, though bleeding, danced and sang while he was being beaten. There is said to be a law in that state which empowers the jury or the court to order that a criminal be given thirty stripes every Monday for a whole year if they seem required. The usual death sentence is hanging! Ugh, how awful! A Negro was hanged in North Carolina because he had stolen a pig jowl from a white man.

"But to more pleasant subjects!—to our second excursion to Cooperville. We traveled first to Heddy Hill, the little place belonging to Cooperville which Hammarsköld had bought as his family's summer place since the iron works were unhealthful at that time of year. It was very small but neat, and they had just got things in order inside and out—that is, had planted a number of fruit trees and flowers round about, when they suddenly had to leave it all. Garden pink grew there like weeds. When we arrived at the works—Cherokee Ford, as it is also called since the area thereabouts had formerly belonged to the Cherokee Indians who forded the river at that place—we set off on the opposite side of the river from the previous time. It was even more beautiful there, the land more varied, with hills and dales, and even a little mountainous; the trees arched completely over the river, and I recalled the descriptions I had read of American rivers, how boats could be hidden under the overhanging foliage, how easy it had been.

"In the middle of the river there is a pretty little islet with similar shores; higher up at the works there is a little waterfall and a dam. In some places the shores were so overgrown that we could make our way forward only with difficulty, had to get down on our knees and be very humble; at other places we would unexpectedly come upon an open space with the finest white sand and enclosed by bushes, almost woven tightly together by vines, among which the pink honeysuckle took the prize. Growing there in great abundance were our blue garden-variety lupines, a kind of white, scentless lily and another sort of flower, very tall with leaves like those of the light yellow lily at home; they were now only buds but they must look magnificent when they are in bloom. The beautiful mountain laurel also adorned this place. After rambling a while longer we returned to our picnic hamper, where we met Charlie Hammarsköld and Mr. Wessman (formerly a servant with the Hammarskölds, now their assistant, pleasant and proper and treated with great friendliness and respect by them) and ate a simple but very pleasant meal.

"Then the walk was resumed when we—Tant, Carl, and I—pressed forward. We found white flowering rhododendron on a cliff overlooking the river and a kind of bush called syringa but with flowers and leaves exactly like our jasmine, though scentless. After walking a while we came upon a saw which seemed to be in completely workable condition, surrounded by piles of boards, but abandoned. We went in and Carl showed me a circular sawblade, which is supposed to be very good. . . .

"On the way back I came upon a magnolia, not a grandiflora, which grows farther south and is said to have flowers as large as plates and an especially strong fragrance. This was a glauca,[3] the flower the size of a tumbler and with such strong fragrance that we could not have it inside the carriage but had to press it at once; we passed Gilky Mountain on the

3 The sweet bay, also called swamp bay

way back and in the shop I came upon a press, rather like my own, bought it and have now had it altered for flower pressing."

Having returned from this pleasant excursion, Rosalie had social and botanical events at Limestone Springs to describe in the same letter to her family in Sweden: "Directly opposite the hotel there is a little white house with green shutters and a flower garden outside. It belongs to one of the state's former governors who is still called Governor Johnson. He has been away all winter, did not return until spring. I have been on a visit to his house together with Miss Crittenden and Hulda. He is a venerable old fellow with long, gray locks, but so huge, so huge, that old man Gren would look quite small and insignificant next to him. He is a widower, and a mulatto, Dorinda, looks after him like a daughter, seems indeed to be the mistress of the house. He has a married daughter who has gone off to Texas to live there with her mother-in-law since her husband, who was twenty-one years old when they were married, has not yet completed his studies. It is not unusual for people to get married before they have left the academies and colleges. There is said to have been a young wife here several years ago whose husband attended school somewhere else. In Georgia Hulda saw someone who used to go out in the morning and amuse herself with her young friends, leaving the cares of her little home to her mother and husband.

"On the eighth of May I ate the first strawberries. Eliza Peronneau had got them from her relatives, and the dear girl thought immediately of me and prepared a bowl for me. They taste like our garden strawberries, and the wild ones also have the same flavor though not quite so strong. On the twenty-first of May came the first cherries; one of the girls had received a basket from home and she too came and gave me some. Yesterday when I was at Tant's, Heddie appeared with some mulberries on a leaf which she had picked in the hotel garden. All during May there have been roses of many kinds in great abundance, including the most delightful tea roses, white, pale pink, pale yellow, and a white with traces of both yellow and red. There is a small but exceedingly beautiful garden at Dr. Otterson's, a veritable rosary. Around the tall trees—acacia, pride of China, hickory, etc.—yellow jasmine, pink honeysuckle, trumpet creeper, and certain kinds of roses entwine themselves, and between the trees are bushes overflowing with roses, all sizes and colors. They have about thirty different kinds of roses there, and there were surely fourteen in the bouquet I brought home with me. The white lilies are now at their most beautiful. I have just received a magnificent stalk of them for my room, a present from the Governor's Dorinda, with five flowers open and three buds. They have filled the whole room with their perfume. Several kinds of verbena also grow in the gardens. And now the white, true jasmine is beginning to bloom. It is quite unlike the ordinary one.

"In deference to the necessity of getting some summer clothes in order, I have been obliged for a time to neglect my flowers. I think, however, that I shall have close to two hundred separate species and duplicates at least of every kind.

"The May Day festival for this year was canceled on account of widespread illness, which the girls did not particularly like—nor did I, who had wished to see the festivities. Then there was a question whether to celebrate the doctor's birthday with a picnic or a party, but in consideration of Major Sims's serious illness and his family's anxiety, it was not thought suitable. He fell ill about three weeks ago of erysipelas. . . . Since I liked the ladies in the family very much, I went over there one morning to inquire after his condition. Tant Hammarsköld came along and we found the house plunged into sorrow since he was believed to be dying. . . . At our departure Sally Sims said, 'Oh Miss Roos, do come back again!' He did not die then; the spark of life flamed up again. I wanted to go back but was prevented by Hulda, who urged me not to because Miss Crittenden said that it was unsuitable, that young women have no business being in a house where a gentleman lies ill, etc. How such pettiness, how such narrowminded prejudices vex me, although in my dependent state I must let myself be guided by them. In this matter America is far worse than Sweden, for a good many harmless things 'won't do' here. After another fortnight's struggle and after everyone began to hope for his recovery, Major Sims died Wednesday evening and on Thursday his family, Mr. and Mrs. Curtis, relatives of Sims, drove down to their plantation, thirteen miles from here, where he was buried the same day. Brandy for internal use had been prescribed by the doctor the whole time(!)."

Rosalie wrote to her brother Emil, 27 May 1852: "In one of my letters I think surely I mentioned that the girls had obtained a piano for their recreation room and I promised to play for them. Some of them have taken especially to dancing, and I have been down several times and played for them; then their mirth filled the room, and at times I have also had to take part in the dance. I have taught them 'väva vadmal' [Weaving Dance], both the regular and the other one, and the former in particular aroused tempestuous approval—they shrieked with delight. I have also introduced the clap anglaise. Their own dances include a so-called cotillion, not at all like ours but rather a kind of quadrille; also a reel, where the couples are arranged as in an anglaise; the latter has some resemblance to our so-called Dagsnäs anglaise. They usually dance now on Friday and Saturday evenings, after school, supper, and prayers."

Rosalie's midsummer letter of 25 June to her mother told anxiously of the approaching examinations, which had given rise to a need to refurbish her summer wardrobe. The girls had to practice a little extra, and the luxuriant vegetation persisted in tempting her to go on botanical excursions: "Mr. Curtis has been very friendly toward me, often inviting me into his study to examine flowers with him, helping me put into order those that I myself have not had time for, always asking me to come in when he has obtained something new and can share it with me.

"I wonder if you can guess what I did a fortnight ago? Nothing less than helping Mrs. Curtis with her baking in order to show her some Swedish pepparkakor; I chose ginger cookies since they were the cheapest, and besides they have neither almonds nor cardamon here. But I had to do four batches to make enough to go around, and they all went at supper on Sunday evening. What do you think, Mama, of so compact a household as this? We now have eighty-one full-time boarders in residence; twelve are teachers, including the principals and Mrs. Curtis; Curtis has four children, and besides the housekeeper two men acting as supervisors, and then all the servants, who nevertheless are not proportionately so many. Two Negresses clean the rooms, which are not swept, however, until the afternoon; two Negroes wait on table, three to four Negresses wash and iron ceaselessly, hard work when it is warm; one Negro does odd jobs outdoors, cleans the public rooms, cleans and fills the lamps, rings the bell, fetches the post, and so on. In addition, a couple in the kitchen, as well as some outside whom I do not know how to account for. Once a week Mr. Humphries and his mule come to deliver supplies.

"If I really survive the examinations, I shall have bright prospects on the other side of those terrible days. Tant Hammarsköld has invited Hulda and me to accompany Heddie when she leaves Limestone in the days following the examinations. It will not be for long, since we do not have vacations here in the summer, but when the examination days are over, the remainder of the week will be given to rest and pleasure.

"You speak of Mlle. Bremer and suggest that I too try to take note of as much as possible. But the difference between us is immense! During the two-year period of her travels in America she had nothing other to do than research, to look about, and to gather information, and to this end she was accorded the help of the natives in the most obliging manner since her name was known throughout the United States. Consider now my situation, restricted to a place like Limestone, so isolated from the world, and with so much to do that I scarcely have the time to call on our good-natured neighbors once a month. And if I should travel, and I were to come to a city, who would know me, who would bother about me?

"You speak of speculating in matches in order to get money for me to travel, but Mama dear, I fear that is a gamble that will go up in smoke. The Captain is supposed to have had commissions from someone in Sweden, but it didn't work out. In the larger cities they are not so expensive, but out in the country here they earn a sizable percent as at home. The boxes are exactly like the round wooden boxes they had at home at one time and they hold about as many, costing five cents, but three boxes sell for ten cents."

Evidently in reply to her father's requests for detailed information about conditions in America, Rosalie cautioned him not to let his hopes rise too high, for she had little time for letter writing; but in a letter of 27 June he nevertheless received a report concerning the cultivation of trees, bushes, and vegetables.

"The wheat was cut about three weeks ago to my great surprise, for I thought at first that it was hay, but they do not trouble themselves with that, instead allowing the poor cattle to wander about in the woods the whole winter and find what fodder they can. Corn requires longer time and is just now coming into flower. It has a splendid appearance, although it is said not to grow very tall here, but in rich soil a horse and rider could make their way through a field of corn without being seen. Because it branches out so much, it is not sown but is planted in small mounds rather distant from one another. . . . The ears are said to be remarkably flavorful when they are roasted. Corn and pork are the Americans' staple foods. They can live day after day on ham, hominy, and corn bread, and these dishes are never absent from the tables of the natives. When fruit is in season many families who do not care for hard work are said to live on fruit, especially blackberries, and cornbread. The season for flowers is past its peak now, especially in the gardens. . . . My sweet peas have begun to bloom, but I fear that the sun is too strong for them. There are still some beautiful things to be seen out in the woods and in the fields.

"The heat has been quite moderate during the month of June, but for a few days the thermometer rose to ninety degrees Fahrenheit, a fairly respectable temperature. Everyone was perspiring, panting, and drinking huge amounts, and in the nights we slept with the windows open as is customary generally as early as May and during rather chilly nights. They think it unhealthful to keep the windows closed. The evenings now are the most suitable time for walking. When the stars light up in the clear blue sky, a refreshing breeze whispers now and then in the treetops and wafts the fragrance of flowers about, the whippoorwill begins his song, the fireflies glow like sparks being quickly extinguished, then it is lovely to go strolling either out in the open or on the pleasant piazzas, and it is difficult to go in and go to bed."

A month later, on 30 July 1852, Rosalie was able to report to her mother that the examinations were finished. "Since I wrote last there have been some diversions in our monotonous life, first the examination days, which thank heavens are now over, and after that, what was much more pleasant: our trip to Columbia Furnace[4] and the Hammarskölds. Mama, I wouldn't for anything want to live through the examination days again! You can well imagine what a trial it would be for me, who have always been such a coward at such times, to appear before so numerous a gathering who did not know me and from whom I therefore could not hope to have any forbearance. When I played the first piece, a fairly easy waltz for four hands with one of my pupils, a beginner, I was so frightened that my heart beat in 6/4 time and I scarcely could find the keys. My poor pupil made out no better for that, and in consequence she too made some mistakes, but since we did not stop but continued straight on, they were not especially noticed, and I was feeling fairly good about it all. A little while later it was again my turn to play. I then took another of my beginning pupils, who had practiced very diligently and for a long time had got up to play every morning before the gong was sounded for arising. Before we went down, we tried our duet on my piano; it went rather well. But imagine my dismay when after having played a few measures, she lost her place completely and stopped, so that I had to show her where she was to play. Made anxious by this, she gets worse and worse, and time after time she stops and I must play alone, which continued throughout the whole piece. . . .

"The days we spent in North Carolina went by all too quickly. Their little home at Columbia Furnace is very simple compared with their Swedish home, but I liked it very much and it seemed very pleasant to me. A pretty, spacious parlor and a room for Heddie had been added on, as well as a guest room. The piazza, which is covered, was used as a dining room, and it was quite delightful to take our meals out there with the beautiful countryside all about. Sunday we went out riding, Hulda, Heddie, and I, in addition to Carl and Mr. Wessman. . . .

4 Iron works located on the Little Catawba River about ten miles downstream from Lincolnton, North Carolina; successfully operated in the early years of the century by John Fulenwider and his son, the works was renovated in 1839 by the High Shoals Manufacturing Company but abandoned in 1854, perhaps while Hammarsköld was associated with it. Lester A. Cappon, "Iron-Making—A Forgotten Industry of North Carolina," *North Carolina Historical Review* 9 (October, 1932), 345.

"I can't quite bring myself to accept the manners of American gentlemen: tilting and rocking in their chairs, putting their feet up on chairs, tables, benches, indeed even on window sills, chewing tobacco ceaselessly and then spitting. At dinner on Monday there was a Dr. Sloan at the Hammarskölds' from Dallas [N.C.], a little town three years old with three hundred inhabitants, and he stayed the whole afternoon. He took his seat next to Tant on the sofa saying: 'I must sit next to you so I can spit through the window.' What do you think of that? And that was one of the most distinguished gentlemen of this place!"

At her father's request Rosalie had inquired of Hjalmar Hammarsköld, the architect in Charleston, if he could possibly have use for her brother Axel, who had just completed his studies at the Technological Institute in Stockholm. She received an affirmative answer and on the fifth of August wrote to her father that he should give the offer serious consideration. She was thrilled at the possibility of her brother's coming over and began deliberating how to find a position for herself nearer Charleston. "I get along very well at Limestone and could hardly do otherwise since everyone is so extremely kind and friendly toward me here, but I look on it almost as a duty to subject myself to the ordeal of a separation and the difficulty of new circumstances if I am to get to see and become acquainted with more of the country in the time that I am staying here.

"I have already mentioned Eliza Peronneau, one of my best pupils, of whom I am very fond. She is seventeen years old, her sister Annie fifteen. They leave Limestone in the fall and probably will not return, for which reason I asked her the other day if their parents did not intend to engage a teacher to complete their education and to give instruction to their twelve-year-old sister still at home. She replied that she thought they would if they could secure someone suitable. I then mentioned to her that I would be leaving Limestone in the fall and had not yet decided where I would be working in the coming year but that I would not be unwilling to spend it in their family although this would still be a secret between us. She was very happy to hear this, embraced me, and said that it was a very delightful secret and that she wished very much it could be so. She was now to write to her parents to hear what they might say. Her father has a rice plantation south of Charleston. . . . These girls have more manners and better taste than is common here among our 'young ladies,' are kind and well brought up, so that I have a good impression of this family."

In her next letter home, 27 August 1852, Rosalie was able to report that the Peronneau family would indeed receive her in their home when her engagement at Limestone came to an end: "The whole business has proceeded so quietly and quickly that no one other than Hulda has had any hint of it. The letter came last Tuesday. Eliza came eagerly and happily with it in her hand, sought me out at Mr. Rosa's, where I was playing chess, signaled to me, and when we both had come half-running into my room she embraced me while she both laughed and wept as she told me what the answer would be. Her mother wrote that she did not want to think of me as a stranger but as a member of the family and sent me her greetings as though to a friend. I had from little Clelia, twelve years old, a letter and some very odd sheets of paper; from Mary, ten years old, 'love' and a bit of rice from the year's harvest. Both the little girls had been very worried until 'the big question' had been decided upon. If ever one could dare judge by appearances as to expectations for the future, it does seem that I join this family under good auspices. There is no doubt in my mind that both the girls are fond of me; Eliza is in a state of bliss and talks of the good times we shall have together, how we are going to study French, paint, play the piano, go riding, botanize, visit the Negro cabins together and try to give instruction to the children and sew clothes for them. This latter touched me the most and speaks well for my little darling's good heart. She claims that she feels I already belong to her, but is now only concerned that Mr. Curtis will disapprove of our arrangements."

These fears were indeed to be confirmed, partly because Curtis regretted not being able to keep Rosalie at the school, partly because he had hoped to have the youngest Peronneau girls come as pupils to Limestone. For Rosalie, however, it was a move that she never needed to regret. It led to a friendship which lasted not only throughout her lifetime but has persisted on both sides for every succeeding generation. In her letter of 23 September to her father she quoted from Mrs. Peronneau's very friendly note in order to reassure him that this position would turn out to be entirely satisfactory. Rosalie took note of the heavy responsibilities she felt in assuming the instruction of the children in all the usual school subjects: "How bitterly and deeply do I often regret my lack of basic knowledge! So did I also at home, but there was little occasion there to feel the lack as much as I do here when I have other instruction to impart and want to do it as thoroughly as possible. Strangest of all, most of them think that I know so much when in fact it is so little, for it is all superficial. How many times have I not wished to have pursued my studies in only one direction! I might then have been able to make excellent progress if I had properly used the ability to cultivate what Providence endowed me with—now, however, all that I know is on closer inspection reduced to naught. The sense of never being able to bring it all together, of never being sure of anything but feeling in every subject only uncertainty, the fear of being wrong, depresses me at times and dispirits me. . . . How incomplete and inadequate is not the instruction that is generally imparted, and how little trouble do not most teachers take to convey thorough knowledge to their pupils! But that is what I know I have tried to do with my own, and I believe that if my teachers had done as much for me, I would have known more than is now the case. I have myself learned a great deal of French this year and discovered many new things in the field of grammar, but nothing is to be gained by complaining about what can no longer be remedied; I must instead be very thankful for what I have, or rather that the little knowledge I have has been able to carry me so far.—But now I really must be allowed to speak of something more pleasant, something that will make you happy, Papa, and that is that I now write English almost entirely without error. . . .

"Although next year will no doubt have its wearisome and lonely moments, it will, however, be good for me as far as speaking the language is concerned, for I will not have daily opportunity to avail myself of my mother tongue. Likewise with respect to a more thorough study of the grammar in which I will now have to give instruction as well as in the history and geography of the country. . . .

"You ask if I have drawn any more pictures. No, no, better to ask: 'My dear child, are you able to keep yourself hale and hearty?' for that is, believe me, difficult enough. If I did not have to think about clothes, I would be truly satisfied, but they never leave me in peace for we are expected always to be well dressed, and were I not to take the responsibility for keeping my clothes in good order, no one else would. It has indeed been difficult this year, when I have had to alter all my dresses, but it doesn't look as though it will be better next year since so much more will be needed, for they are very elegant in Charleston. I certainly will not enter into competition of any kind in this matter, for my taste is simple, but one must give thought to those one lives with and I wish to come no more into notice for a careless toilet than for a grand one. I shall gladly do my level best to sew whatever may be needed in order to cut down expenses, and so far I have made out pretty well, but we shall see how much further this can continue.

"Your travel plans are indeed excellent, Papa,—that is, so far as their being agreeable is concerned, and no one could wish for their fulfillment more than I. But 'much money' will be required, and I fear that I should have to stay here a long time if I were to wait until I had gathered together such a considerable purse for travel. . . .You have only to consider that passage between Charleston and New York costs $25, New York and Liverpool $175,—those are, believe me, not small amounts."

Later that autumn, on 7 November 1852, Rosalie wrote of an addition to the Curtis family of a little girl born just a week before: "They now have six children, the oldest nine years, so that the mother has enough to keep her busy. In general families are large here, twelve to fourteen children is fairly usual. Dr. Otterson's seven daughters make a goodly number!

"I have thought many times of telling you about my little watch, which is in fine fettle. It kept time nicely, but when I was in a great hurry to dust one time, it fell to the floor and would not run. You can imagine my grief, but Sally Giles sent it to Union and I had it repaired and cleaned, so that it really glistened after having been relieved of its century-old accumulation. But that too cost $5. The girls take great delight in it and cannot admire it enough; they want to ~~go~~ travel[5] to Sweden to get one like it. You see from my mistake in the last line that it sometimes happens that I mix English expressions in with my Swedish. That is often the case with Hulda and me without our being aware of it, but we laugh heartily when we notice it. Sometimes when I am writing, I have to ponder whether the expression is correct. I am afraid that we are going to speak a funny sort of Swedish when we come home. When, when will that be?!?"

Addressing herself in a general letter to "all my dear ones," Rosalie wrote on 16 November 1852: "Since I last wrote to you we have had a quite noticeable change in the weather, which was transformed really at one stroke from summer heat to winter cold . . . and freezing now with cold, we shout for wood, wood! As winter weather it would indeed be the most agreeable imaginable, if only the rooms were more tightly sealed, but since the houses are built only for the summers, the wind blows in everywhere. The natives do not suffer nearly as much as do we spoiled northerners. They no doubt feel the cold and shiver but endure it nevertheless better than we; they make a fire and then keep the doors and sometimes the windows open, gathering as close as they can to the fire. When you go on a visit, you are offered a chair near the fire and the whole company sits in a circle around the fireplace. Many keep the windows in their bedrooms open at night the whole winter through, but I pile on the blankets as much as possible so as not to freeze. It is all to the good now to be on friendly terms with the servants if you want wood. Our washerwoman comes up every now and then with a bundle of 'lightwood' as a present for Hulda and me, and depend on it, it is very welcome. This wood consists of pine which is so full of resin that it almost sticks to the

---

5 In the original, Rosalie struck through the word *gå*, cognate of English "go" and pronounced like it but limited in this context to mean "go on foot"; she replaced it with *fara*, "to travel" (as across an ocean, etc.).

fingers; without it, it is almost impossible to get the chestnut wood to burn.

"So much for weather and wood. We shall rise now to a discussion of the recent election of 'members in the Senate' and 'Legislature' and finally of the President. In connection with these elections there has been, as they say here, much 'excitement.' These elections took place last month, and since many of the girls' fathers were candidates, I heard a great deal about them, and even felt some of the excitement myself as we waited to hear the results. The proceedings, however, are not always very open and honest, for many of the candidates travel about for several months in advance to secure votes, which is called 'to go electioneering.' A Major Giles, whose daughter is one of my pupils, was a candidate and supposed that he would certainly get into the Senate, but his opponent won, so it is claimed, after having bought votes for several hundred dollars. Giles's sons felt deep bitterness toward the winner, and there was talk that one of them in a moment of rage pointed his pistol at the latter, but when he was held back by one of those present, he missed his aim, whereupon the pistol went off and the bullet went through his own father's hat. That was not half bad, however, for young Giles had earlier been seized by a relative of the victorious candidate and been given a severe caning originally intended for someone else. He had then taken out his pistol to shoot his assailant but was prevented, as I have already mentioned. The bullet went through his father's hat but without injuring him. That is only a little sample of how brute force is at times the law here. Sally Giles wept bitter tears over her father's defeat. You perhaps already know how the presidential election turned out. I can add only that General Pierce . . . has the majority on his side.

"After politics we shall have a bit of romance. This was so remarkable a day that I believe I must begin at the beginning. By mistake Lorenz rang the bell for reveille an hour too early, that is at 5 o'clock, while it was still completely dark. I could not understand the cause, especially since a great deal of movement and noise followed, and I began almost to fear that fire had broken out, but that guess was contradicted by the laughter and merriment that followed. When I peeked out, I saw the girls running up and down the corridors quite thinly clad, laughing and shouting and persuaded to return to bed only after repeated commands from the teachers. They took the occasion as so excellent for a lark and for creating a disturbance that they were quite unwilling to let it slip through their fingers. But the aftermath came at the breakfast table, consisting of demerits for all those who had had a part in the escapade. After breakfast some of the 'young ladies' were heard to grumble a bit, but all that soon died away in the course of their lessons.

"At dinner time something else occurred. One of the 'young ladies,' Cicely Atkinson, who graduated this summer, was missing, and there was reason to believe that her disappearance had something to do with some buggies that had been visible for a short while at the hotel but then had quickly disappeared. And that was indeed how matters really stood. A couple of women in the neighborhood had gone to a shop three miles away and there had met some young men who, however, soon departed. On the way home they met them again, but then a young woman with a veil pulled down over her face was sitting in a chaise and the perspiring horse dashed away as fast as it could. Our ladies did not have time to draw any conclusions before they had passed, but afterwards a couple of other chaises showed up with young gentlemen who when asked if they had stolen a girl answered, 'Yes, yes, hurrah!' and tossed their hats into the air. The plan was bold but it succeeded superbly, though you will of course understand what consternation it aroused here. The Curtises were taken completely by surprise and set out after the fugitives. But when they stopped a few miles from here to make inquiries, they discovered that the lovers, or rather the newlyweds, had just departed after having been married by a priest who had come out to meet them. Mr. Pagan, the bridegroom, had been courting her since the beginning of the year, but her father, who considered her to be still too young to take so important a step, had set himself in opposition. She had had her sixteenth birthday only a few days before the marriage. Mr. P. had then suggested an elopement to her, to which, however, she had at first given a negative answer but had finally allowed herself to be persuaded and had even attempted to carry it out when she went home after the examinations, but had then been pursued, overtaken, and brought back by the father. In order to divert her thoughts she was sent back to school, but here she found a still better opportunity. She had been corresponding the entire time with Mr. Pagan and thus knew of his arrival and on that same day had been seen gazing out toward the road without anyone's having taken particular notice of it. Finally some buggies arrived with the young gentlemen, and a brother of one of the girls came here to call on his sister, at which time he gave Cicely a letter. She put on her hood, and almost directly outside the gate here she got up into the buggy which took her away. Her sister missed her, and when Mr. Curtis, who had been told of the meeting by one of the neighbor women, asked if any of the girls was missing, she came forward weeping and said: 'I have been looking in vain for Cicely for a long time.'

To everyone's dismay it was now apparent that Cicely had indeed fled. The episode made a painful and unpleasant impression on me, and I felt sorry for both the misguided girl and her poor parents. But the case is not so unusual here—it is the third elopement that has taken place in this region in the last two months—and since the father is said to have obtained his wife in the same manner, he is not likely to be too badly worked up over it. They are said to be reconciled now, and the newlyweds have been home to visit her parents.—To get married here does not require as much as at home. They do not trouble themselves about banns, wedding, a house to live in, or furniture. If they have reached an agreement, the parties betake themselves to a priest and then afterwards they travel or establish themselves in a hotel until they find it appropriate to set up housekeeping.

"The first wedding or marriage which I heard about and at which I also was present seemed to me extremely peculiar. It was Mr. Rosa's and Miss Tooker's wedding. They were engaged when I arrived, but she was so very fearful that this would become known that they scarcely talked to each other when anyone else was present. There were, however, not so few people who were in on the secret, but all the same most of the girls and the servants as well as the neighbors still knew nothing of it the day before their marriage. They knew no doubt that Mr. Rosa was going to be married, that his bride was here, but as to who it was their opinions were divided. When at the request of the bride Hulda and I invited Miss Armstrong on the morning of the wedding day to be present at the marriage ceremony, she only thought that we were having a bit of fun. She was nevertheless convinced when she came down to the parlor where all the girls had gathered and to which Mr. Curtis brought the bride and Mrs. Curtis the bridegroom, and where Dr. Curtis joined them in wedlock. Afterwards there was a breakfast, and when it was over, the newlyweds journeyed to New York where her mother lives. They had no worries about where they would live, do not have even one silver spoon but are engaged here as teachers and will reside in the rooms that Hulda and I had last year. Voilà tout! They will be staying on here next year."

In a letter of 27 February 1853 to her sister and brother-in-law, Leonie and Thure von Nackreij, Rosalie was able to tell of some pleasant times she had enjoyed at the school: "Rosa's birthday was also remembered and celebrated in America. At midday one of the girls came up with a tray upon which were a pair of undersleeves, a collar, and a nice little verse. On inquiry I learned that it was from Eliza P. In the evening I was invited to Isabella Cunningham's for supper, where some of the teachers and girls had assembled. We have great fun at these supés, I assure you.

Imagine a room furnished with two tables, two chairs, one large bed, and two or three trunks, and within the same a dozen or more girls. Some sit on chairs, trunks, and tables, while at least a dozen lie on the bed, which serves the same purpose as did the Roman couches. Set out on the table are cold chicken on a plate, butter on a saucer, a cake and biscuits and pepparkakor on paper. After the hostess has urged them to partake of whatever might taste best to them, everyone helps herself, and for this the aids provided by Nature are supplemented by a knife that is very much in demand. In general, appetites are extremely good, mirth and laughter instead of spirits enliven the company, but while the merriment is at its peak, a peremptory bell rings, in consequence of which the picked bones are quickly discarded, biscuits and cakes are stuffed into pockets, fingers and mouths are wiped with handkerchiefs to prepare for a hasty farewell kiss, and then all rush back to their rooms. I received from Isabella a deluxe edition of Byron's works, extremely beautiful. . . . Hulda gave me a beautiful collar, Miss Wilson a pair of knitted cuffs and a little 'friendly note.' "

In a letter sent from the Peronneau plantation "Dungannon" to "all my dear ones" on 24 January 1853, Rosalie looked back to the beginning of December when Governor Johnson gave a farewell party to "all Limestone residents": "His little dwelling was even prettier than usual and had been placed entirely at our disposal from attic to cellar, as he expressed it. I had not seen before the rooms in the second story, which are quite pretty and well furnished but do not interconnect, only having doors opening on the little hallway, which is, however, quite attractive with its papered walls and its floor furnished with rugs, as are the stairs. Tea was served with wafers, sandwiches, and waffles after we had greeted the host, and afterwards we made conversation as best we could with the guests. We tried to encourage the girls to start some games, but that was a thankless effort, for most neither understood nor wanted to understand anything—they were quite impossible. Hulda, Miss Wilson, and Eliza Peronneau dressed up as gypsies and sang some songs to guitar accompaniment, which pleased the company a great deal. About ten o'clock we had supper, which was truly splendid for being at Limestone. It was served in two rooms in the lower story. The tables were quite handsome with large 'custard stands' (resembling what we call <u>servanter</u>, with many round shelves decreasing in size upward), decked out with white paper and flowers and bearing a quantity of cups and glasses containing cloudberry gelatin, custard (something like our lemon crème), and syllabub (sugar, cream, and some arrack, whipped until thick). Everything for the supé had been placed out on the tables: butter, bread, ham, smoked meat, goose, turkey, several kinds of cakes, some of them glacé, prunes, raisins and almonds, apples, walnuts, chestnuts, peanuts (a kind of nut which grows in the ground and tastes almost like raw peas), in addition to wines and liqueurs, which are called cordials. Shortly after supper was over, around midnight, we made our way home."

VI

DEPARTURE FROM LIMESTONE; CHRISTMAS AT COLUMBIA FURNACE

Rosalie and Hulda had been invited to spend Christmas at Columbia Furnance in North Carolina with the Hammarsköld family. Rosalie described their departure from Limestone in a letter to her father dated 21 December 1852: "All during the month the school at Limestone was being dispersed since one or another of the pupils left it nearly every day, and finally there remained only the girls whose parents lived in 'the Low Country,' and whom Mr. Curtis drove to Columbia and Charleston. . . .

"Since everyone at Limestone had treated me with exceptional good will it was with feelings of both gratitude and sadness that I left them. My pecuniary affairs were also properly taken care of. Dear Franz took charge of mine as well as of Hulda's. It also fell to my lot as a quite pleasant surprise to find a larger amount than I had counted on, for instead of $300 I got $350 and an additional $25 for the extra lessons. I would have liked to have a safe place to deposit the $200 which I had intended to set aside from the year's salary. Let us see if I can save up enough so that I can realize in the following year all my travel plans. But—but—it will be heavy going, for my plans are extensive . . . In the morning of the 16th Mr. Curtis and his family set out with a couple of teachers and about 30 young ladies. They had thirteen wagons, and Dr. Curtis himself rode horseback in order to be able to oversee everything. The day was rainy and unpleasant, the roads horrible.

"On the first day they were to reach Yorkville, twenty miles from Limestone, and from there travel by train to Columbia and then to Charleston. Their things had been sent ahead, and along with them had gone Hulda's and my large trunks to be held for us at York. Let's hope we see them there! It would be a cruel joke if they should be lost, but that is quite possible.

"Last Friday morning we three Swedes left Limestone in the company of Mr. Hammarsköld. The roads were wretched beyond all description after more than a week's unceasing rain, and the streams and rivers were flooded. We had several small waterways to cross over besides 'Muddy Creek,' a not so little stream where the water got up into the buggy, and also Broad River, which we crossed on a rickety ferry. It is really a quite nasty stretch especially when the water has risen, which was the case when the girls left Limestone. The water rose into the wagons, and Mr. Curtis's buggy had been lost on the way back from York. The horse had drowned, and the Negro had scarcely been able to save himself by swimming.

"I would have liked to see you, Mutter dear, if you had been with us across 'Muddy Creek,' which looked quite dreary although we kept in good spirits when the water gradually rose and finally gave our feet a cold bath although we had lifted them as high as we could. Once up on dry land the buggy had to be bailed out, and poor Franz, who had endured the worst flooding because of his long legs, dried his lower extremities in the sunshine. The distance from Limestone here is about 38 miles, and since it was already past ten when we left Limestone, I did not think we would make it in one day, but we arrived at eight o'clock, which was quite marvelous when you consider the dreadful roads where the mud rose up as high as the axle. The horses in this country have a rough time of it. They did not get either to eat or to rest for the whole journey although they had been going for two days.

"This Christmas, my second in America, is decidedly superior to the first, for I am spending it in the company of fellow countrymen and the dearest friends I have on this side of the ocean. These happy and refreshing days will soon enough have sped by, however, for we leave Columbia Furnace for Charleston as early as January 2. After having been obliged as much by work as by the ringing of bells to keep bustling about, it feels both strange and peaceful to live here in the most thoroughgoing restfulness and to work only as much as is pleasing to oneself and, what is almost stranger still, to hear only Swedish spoken. I have still not been able to convince myself that I have really left Limestone for good; I feel as though I will soon be returning there to begin once again my regular tasks.

"The Negroes had a week off during Christmas which they used for visiting and dancing. Happier, more carefree people than the blacks can scarcely be imagined. They came one evening to the Hammarskölds' and danced on the piazza, and we stood watching their dance, which is quite unique. It is done almost exclusively with the feet, which possess great nimbleness and muscular strength; they move them with unbelievable suppleness while standing almost on one spot. After a time they almost fall into a kind of delirium, as it were; their movements become faster and faster and they begin to run about, bowing, watching the feet of the other dancers, fanning the air with their hats, etc. They dance best and most lightly when barefoot. The men's dance is more entertaining to watch than the women's, whose movements can't be seen because of their skirts, but they look like puppets being tugged up and down on strings. One of the black gentlemen was a particularly great dancer. He was dressed in a fine frock coat and pants, silk vest and pleated shirt, and danced so that his face was beaded with perspiration—he was utterly indefatigable. They played the violin, banjo (an instrument resembling the guitar), and sang. It was amusing to see them although I cannot deny that these dark figures with the whites of their eyes and their shining rows of teeth in sharp contrast looked ghastly enough in the half darkness. When they finished dancing, they expressed thanks with special satisfaction for the pleasure they had enjoyed. On Christmas Day I looked out the window and I saw several elegant gentlemen strolling on the highway, and was just about to express my astonishment when I noticed that they were black."

In her letter addressed to "all my dear ones," Rosalie wrote, "In the morning of 2 January we left our little Sweden to travel by wagon to York, where the railroad begins. The beautiful weather in which we had rejoiced in the morning had been succeeded by rain continuing the whole day, although we were not inconvenienced by it since we had a covered vehicle. Our little company consisted of Hulda, Heddie, and the undersigned escorted by Messrs. Franz Hahr and Carl Hammarsköld. The roads were worse than dreadful, and the gentlemen, who had provided two young horses for the light buggy in which we rode, had to unhitch them a couple of times and take those that we had for our wagon which were strong and sturdy enough to make it up a couple of hills, whereas theirs refused to budge. At York, a little town with gardens between the houses, the streets, which are not paved, were just as deep in mud. We got out at a hotel where we were expected and where rooms had been prepared for us since Miss [Johanna] Boström, the Hammarskölds' former housekeeper, is now employed there. During the night it snowed and a strong wind blew so that when we awoke in the morning the whole landscape had a quite Nordic appearance."

After changing trains at Chester, the company arrived in the evening at Columbia: "This capital city of South Carolina is quite beautiful and is said to be really splendid especially in spring because of the many beautiful gardens. The streets are 30, 40, and 50 feet wide with trees planted on both sides. We saw the site of the new State House[1] which Hjalmar Ham-

---

1 The cornerstone for the State House, a huge building in the Greek style, was laid in December, 1851. One year later the state commission reported that work was progressing rapidly, "giving the public the cheapest and most magnificent public building in the United

marsköld will build, and were also within a garden owned by a Frenchman. . . . He was thoroughly delighted when we spoke with him in French and took us into an orangery where he showed us some beautiful plants: a banana tree, several camellias and cacti in bloom, a tall Brazilian plant with large crimson flowers, magnificent color; in addition an alligator three feet long which he kept in a box covered with wire. He gave me a cactus shoot that had a few flowers open and promised me a very beautiful bouquet if I came there in the spring.

"We were quite anxious in the morning that we might not get to the station in good time since our gentlemen friends were a little dilatory, and the train was to leave before daylight. But fortunately we got on board and were well stowed away in the small comfortable sofas. The car was filled with passengers, and we set out at a moderate speed. In those places where there is a certain amount of danger of leaving the rails, such as in passing over rivers, gullies, and marshes, the speed is reduced. Most of the time the road goes through woods. . . . We arrived at Charleston at three o'clock after having covered 120 miles."

Momentarily concerned that no one had come to meet her, Rosalie looked about, then saw Eliza and Nannie Peronneau, who had come to the city with their father, rushing to greet her, and coming from the opposite direction was Hjalmar Hammarsköld, ready with a cart and carriage to take her and her things temporarily to his house. The next day she set out to go shopping on King Street. "It has several beautiful shops, but all are surpassed by a new one, Kerrison's,[2] which really deserves to be seen. The whole building, which is quite large, contains only goods for sale, probably worth millions. The store is very large, 270 feet long; the carved ceiling is supported by beautifully ornamented columns and is furnished with a number of beautiful cast iron chandeliers with milk glass globes for gas lights. One goes into the store and down very long aisles with mahogany counters on either side, and in front of them are shelves and drawers for the goods. Everything needed for the toilet, for women as

---

States," but in May, 1854, when the foundation was complete and the walls were well above ground, cracks were found that Hammarsköld, the architect, "could not explain." He was replaced on the report of the use of inferior materials and of poor workmanship. The building was not completed until 1907. George A. Buchanan, Jr., "Government: Municipal, State and Federal," in *Columbia, Capital City of South Carolina 1786–1936*, ed. Helen K. Hennig (Columbia, S.C., 1936), p. 61. A slightly different version states that before the new building had reached the first story "it was found to have settled from its ponderous weight." D. P. Robbins, *Historical and Descriptive Sketch . . . of Columbia, S.C.* (Columbia, S.C.)

2 Located at the corner of King and Hasel Streets and said to be the world's first department store.

well as for men, is here, but each and every kind has its separate department. . . . The entrance consists of four large glass doors, and immediately behind is a semicircular counter with glass drawers containing gloves of all kinds. At the back of the room, a few steps covered with costly rugs rise to a little room built like an alcove, where silk curtains and rugs in brilliant colors are draped to wonderful effect when one enters this immense store. It gives the impression of being a reception hall at the rear of which has been installed the sovereign's throne. At about the middle of the room on the right side is a section set off by a railing like that which encloses an altar, and within there is a stove with a cheerful fire. This area is for the bookkeepers. In addition, the store is heated by several freestanding iron stoves. Along the length of the counters there are small round stools, similar to piano stools, fixed to the floor, for the comfort of the customers; they are made of cast iron and covered in dark red velvet. . . . When lighted up this store is said to be especially magnificent. Don't you think that this store surpasses everything you have imagined of this kind?. . .

"Charleston is not so very small in area, for a little garden is attached to nearly every house and every family has a house, maybe several, at their disposition. Many of them are very beautiful, and the piazzas and verandas which adorn the houses and at times provide a lattice for vines, give them a picturesque appearance. The piazzas, usually enclosed by green jalousies, make cool resorts for the city dwellers. You can tell you are in the South both by the buildings and the vegetation surrounding them. . . . What adds very much to the charm of these dwellings are the beautiful entrance halls, papered and carpeted (as are the stairs), and lighted in the evenings. Gas illumination is very common. It is particularly handy in only having to be turned up and lighted. What a difference between Limestone and its environs and Charleston! It is as though they were scarcely the same country, so different are they in topography as well as with respect to the people and their customs.

"Residences here are really quite pleasant. You enter the parlor, which is always furnished with a beautiful rug and a smaller and most costly one before the fireplace, which looks quite inviting with its glowing coals on the little grate enclosed in lattice work. Above the mantel there is often a mirror, and on the mantel are also some precious objects: beautiful candlesticks, vases, and various small bric-a-brac. In front of the fireplace, usually in a semicircle: small armchairs, rocking chairs, and ordinary chairs, all covered in shiny horsehair, looking like silk gabardine. In addition, there is usually a table or two with some handsome books and daguerreotypes, which are never absent in an American home. Often there is also a piano as well as small costly pieces of furniture often in the Chinese style. On coming to someone's house, you ring the bell and the gate is opened."

The Hammarskölds exerted themselves to make Rosalie's stay in Charleston as agreeable as possible: "A couple of times we went to the theater to see the so-called Bateman children,[3] two comely youngsters, girls about 10 to 12 years old, who appeared in several plays and acted remarkably well. They were especially sweet in a play called 'The Young Couple,' presumably written exclusively for them. I saw them also in scenes from Shakespeare's 'Richard III,' in which the one played Richard, the other Richmond. Their acting was really remarkable, but the roles were not suited for children. The after pieces were usually farces of a quite low taste, but were nevertheless relished by the audience. Imagine my surprise when among these I recognized 'Löjliga mötena,'[4] performed in pure burlesque style. The noise and the applause in the theater were extremely unpleasant. Entr'actes are not permitted, the audience expressing its displeasure with them by raising a din." The Hammarskölds gave a party one evening: "Most of our countrymen living in the city were there and those natives who make up their circle of friends. . . . We danced to the piano, and although there was little room to move about in, the dancing was lively, consisting chiefly of françaises, a polka or two, waltzes, gallopades, and a schottische, something between a polka and a mazurka. None of us Swedes could dance with the Americans. I tried three times with Mr. Karp—but in vain, and Hulda had the same fate. Finally we danced 'väva vadmal' [Weaving Dance]. Between dances champagne, fruits, and confections were handed around, and several times coffee and tea, sandwiches made of different things, cakes, and wafers. At two o'clock the party broke up, and I believe everyone was pleased with the evening, but certainly it would not have been so lively if the hosts had been American.

"Saturday noon we went to see the exhibition in natural magic by Professor Anderson, 'the great magician.' He was really very clever and was assisted by two small boys, one of whom he magnetized so that he kept a horizontal position in the air supporting himself only with one arm on a cane. It was beautiful but awful. Probably the child had some other support, however—for example, steel wires not visible to the audience." In the evenings there was music, or they played "kille" or whist. But soon

3 Kate (b. 1842) and Ellen Bateman; Kate was later well known for her leading roles in Shakespeare productions in New York and London.
4 Literally, "Ridiculous Encounters," a one-act farce first performed in Sweden in 1814, based on F. B. Hoffmann's comic opera *les Rendez-vous bourgeois*.

these happy days came to an end, and it was time to leave. Hulda departed for Orangeburg, where she had been engaged as a music teacher in a girls' school,[5] and Rosalie made her way to the Peronneau family at "Dungannon."[6]

5 Orangeburg Female College, founded by its principal, I. S. K. Legaré, a Presbyterian minister. The school closed in 1861, and the property was later sold to members of the Claflin family of Massachusetts who replaced the buildings and established a college for Negroes that still bears the family name.

6 Plantation located about eighteen miles south of Charleston—that is, slightly south of present-day Rantowles on State Highway 17 west of the Atlantic Coastline Railroad. As Rosalie explains in later letters, the plantation was rented from Judge George W. Logan while Peronneau was in the process of restoring his own recently acquired plantation, "Standyard."

VII

A HOME IN THE SOUTH

In a letter dated 3 February 1853 from "Dungannon" to her mother and sister, Rosalie wrote: "I am now beginning to feel at home and have very pleasant accommodations. My room is large and attractive with a little garden recently laid out just below my window. The room is furnished with a number of conveniences with which a Limestone teacher has not been spoiled, such as rugs, bookcase, bureau, wardrobe, cabinets, a desk, and an armchair. I was received by everyone with the warmest cordiality. Mr. Peronneau himself came in to fetch me, and the rest of the family were all waiting outside to greet me. As further evidence of their cordiality I can mention four flower pots placed in my room so that I might be greeted there by something I loved: a geranium, a hyacinth, a citrina, and violets. In addition, they had put aside for me a branch with oranges grown in the vicinity. Wasn't that kind! The same evening I arrived, warm water for a foot bath was carried up to my room, and Mrs. P. has asked me to say when I wish to bathe, for I am then to have a small tub brought into my room."

Apart from a routine established for work and rest, Rosalie herself was to decide how the children's lessons were to be organized, not a simple task since their ages ranged from six to eighteen years, and in addition to the Peronneau children there were two others not in the original plans. "Mr. Peronneau wants me to arrange the study hours so that I will have time myself to read since I ought to read Walter Scott in English, Shakespeare, and God alone knows what else. All of his books are at my disposal, and if there are any others I wish to have, I am only to ask and he will try to secure them for me. If the children are the least disobedient, I am to report it to him, for he wants me to enjoy my teaching. He was very concerned at first about my feeling at home and urged me not to be too modest.

"One day we strolled to his plantation which is close by but has not yet been built upon so that he is renting here. He took me all around, showed me the rice threshing, the finished rice, the machine for cleaning it, the fields, the ditches, etc."

Very soon, in February 1853, Rosalie was ready to describe to her father the members of the Peronneau household: "You perhaps would like to know a little about the people who make up this family. 1. Mr. Peronneau, a man between 40 and 50, vigorous, is out on his plantation the whole day, cheerful, industrious, and good natured. He is not rich, for he still is in debt for his property, which he bought a few years ago when it had fallen into disrepair; but by hard work and perseverance he has greatly improved it. Last year was the first that he could count on for a return. The rice planters depend entirely on the year's harvest, and this crop is very dependent upon the weather. Thus they may have considerable income one year, perhaps nothing at all another year. He has about sixty Negroes, who in themselves make up a not inconsiderable fortune, but who also require not so little for their sustenance. It is no small thing to clothe and feed so many. They all have pleasant, newly constructed houses, where two families live together, but with three rooms for each and separate entrances.

"2. Mrs. Peronneau is a remarkable woman, truly the mistress of her household. In her is to be seen none of the ordinary southern indolence and sloth, but she is constantly in motion, taking care of the children, the household, and the Negroes. She has had a good education but has no particular talents, is what they here call intelligent, which is highly valued, and she also is well read. One often finds in America good native intelligence improved through reading; talent and taste are more infrequent but are highly valued. Mrs. Peronneau was first married to a Mr. Parker before she became Mrs. Peronneau, and had two sons by him. The elder, William Parker, owns a cotton plantation in the vicinity, is married, and has three children who even on the coldest days run about outdoors with open collars, short sleeves, and without shoes and stockings. He is 26 years old, a good-looking fellow with a pleasant disposition. The younger son, Edward, I have not seen although he is said to have seen me when he passed through Charleston on his way to Georgia, where he owns property. He is a widower; his little two-year-old daughter Anna, a lively brunette with large black eyes and dark brown curly hair, is being reared here and naturally is the whole family's pet. As soon as she sees me she comes and takes my hand, leads me to the piano, saying, 'Pay the piano.'

"3. You already know something about Eliza. She is now in Charleston, for relatives and friends considered it imperative that she be out 'in company,' so that she has spent a couple of weeks there for pleasure's sake. She has a good head and is in addition very sweet and darling, 18 years old. 4. Anna, 16 years old, is growing up to be a truly beautiful girl. She is not as quick to learn as is Eliza but there is much tenacity in her character. She too is good and amiable, with a quiet and modest demeanor. 5. Clelia, 12 years old, but as tall as Eliza, whom she closely resembles in

The principal recipients of Rosalie's letters: *This page,* Olof Gustaf Roos and Ulrika Roos, her father and mother; *opposite page,* Axel Roos and Leonard Roos, her brothers.

Limestone Female High School, from a lithograph based on a drawing by Rosalie Roos.

Friends in America: *Left,*
Eliza Mathewes, ca. 1870,
and, *below,* her daughter,
Clelia McGowan, in
Charleston, 1886.

"Tant" Hedda Hammarsköld with her children Carl and Heddie, from
a reproduction of a sketch by Maria Rohl made in the early 1840s.

Wedding portrait of Professor Knut Olivecrona and Rosalie Roos, 1857.

appearance. There is in her character more laziness and indolence than in her sisters, but she is remarkable for her even disposition and amusing ways. She has much humor. 6. Mary, 10 years old, a little lively, sensible youngster, who learns quickly and wants to learn everything. Unlike the others, she has light hair and dark eyes, which look particularly intelligent. 7. Henry, 8 years old, a sturdy, sunny boy who always has his lessons prepared even though he is not quick to learn them. He is a good shot, is out with his gun every moment he is free, can shoot a snipe in flight. 8. James, 6 years old, Mama's pet, being the youngest and in delicate health, is small and blonde; he is only occasionally in the schoolroom. Besides these I have among my pupils Essie Habersham, a 13-year-old girl with a rather good head and studious, but a little boisterous and blunt in her manner. . . .

"In your last letter, Papa, you include a little lecture on the subject of my sentimentality, but I can in good conscience assure you that I really do not suffer from that fault. . . . On the other hand, I must admit to sensitivity taken too far, indeed to touchiness. But even I now begin to feel a crust around my heart, . . . as the skin toughens from hard work, as the tender pliant stalk is encased in bark. I suffer neither so easily nor so bitterly as before, but neither do I feel joy, that indescribable feeling of happiness. . . .

"As you quite rightly noted in your last letter, time is almost less my own here than it was in Limestone. There, I could withdraw from the society of others when my duties required. Here, however, I belong to the family, and when it assembles in the evening, I can hardly absent myself from them and spend the evening in my room, especially when they have guests, as is often the case. Living here is more pleasant . . . it is more like home; I give my mite to promote the general well-being, and I find myself to be the object of the concern and solicitude of others. Mrs. P. came up just this evening to see to my fire and brought some coals in a shovel herself to get it going properly. Mr. Peronneau is so extremely kind and really tries to pamper me; it is as though he wants to show me off when guests come. He is very fond of music and I am obliged always to play for him in the evening. . . . I had heard so much said about governesses and their position in private homes that it was not without feelings of trepidation that I entered my new home, preparing myself for the worst. I was all the more delightfully surprised, therefore, when I encountered the opposite. I feel no oppressive dependence whatsoever . . . even the friends and relatives of the family show me as much respect and friendliness as if I were in my own home."

A Home in the South

On a visit to Charleston in early February to attend a concert given by the Norwegian virtuoso violinist Ole Bull, Rosalie learned that a box for her had just arrived by ship from Sweden. In her letter of 23 January 1853 to her mother and sister, Rosalie described her not unalloyed joy. "But as no happiness is ever unmixed, so it was when I then opened the box, for a whole lot of things were mildewed. The boots, for which I thank you, dear Mutter, so very much, were helped by drying. They were very welcome, for I had just run out of shoes and on my visit to Charleston had had to buy a pair of cloth boots for $3. That is high, but still they were very well made; instead of being laced, they are made of a rubber material which stretches when pulled on and then fits tightly around the foot. They are attractive and next to them Källström's seem quite clumsy; it is like the difference between an elegant lady and a servant girl. Our simple cobbler has not improved since I last saw him; I also wondered if it is now the custom at home to have both boots for the same foot since the first pair I was going to put on were that way. Dear, sweet Mutter, don't be offended by my joking and don't grumble about my being fussy, for truth to tell, I am really pleased to have them; in any case they save me $12. If anything more is sent to me, it ought to come by direct shipment because it is difficult to avoid damage on a long voyage. . . .

"To get here, one has to cross the Ashley River, which flows right outside the city, on a large, excellent ferry powered by steam. On the way home we encountered on this ferry another carriage and in it acquaintances, relatives of Mrs. Peronneau's, who wanted us to accompany them home and spend the night at their plantation, only about four miles from the city. Mr. Peronneau was much inclined to this, for it would turn dark before we could reach home. . . . Mr. Parker's plantation is quite beautiful; it is on the Ashley, which at high water forms small pools in the vicinity of the dwellings. It was pleasant and comfortable and after a while we sat down to dinner consisting of venison, potted pigs' feet, hogshead cheese, salmon, rice, and sweet potatoes. In the morning Mr. Peronneau went out with me to show me some magnificent oaks and the cotton processing. On Wednesday morning we continued homeward but at one place had to turn around and take another road because a huge tree had been blown down across the road. . . . When we arrived home, I saw a little baby alligator that Henry had killed. It was an ell[1] long, spotted in brown and yellow,

---

1 A Swedish measure equal to about 23⅓ inches. The Swedish *aln* (cf. Lat. *ulna*) was based on the distance from the elbow to the finger tips; the English and America ell, about 45 inches long, was measured from the shoulder.

long and narrow. The other day I saw a 'cutter,' a kind of tortoise. It was about two ells long, eight inches wide [*sic*], had a dark thick shell and avery ugly, yellow and black toadlike head which it stuck out when irritated. Its bite is dangerous; it lives together with alligators in their holes, and its meat is said to be delicious. There is said to be 'plenty' of alligators in the rice fields, some of them as much as ten feet long. Their tails are very strong and can knock a man down. Mosquitoes are now becoming evident but have so far not been at all bad. There are flies the year round and servants always stand at the dining table and whisk them away with a fan made of peacock feathers."

The Roos family in Sweden had already read a translation of *Uncle Tom's Cabin* when in a letter dated 4 April 1853 Rosalie reported to her father from "Dungannon": "I have at last been able to get hold of a copy of 'Uncle Tom's Cabin' and just begun to read it. This book cannot be bought in Charleston. No bookseller has it for sale. We have had to borrow it from Mrs. Peronneau's sister, and Eliza read it through in one day and in consequence has halfway become an abolitionist. She is the only Carolinian whom I have heard to dislike slavery and believe it unjust. Otherwise the slave owners and others too—yes, our own countrymen— think that it is ordained by God and will prevail into eternity. Eliza and I were just on the point the other day of quarreling with a Dr. Matthews[2] on the subject. He tried every way he could to disparage Mrs. Stowe and said that he had written something to belittle her book which he wanted to send us. Eliza began the controversy and I kept silent as usual, for I remember Papa's saying that if I cannot contribute something good by speaking it is better to remain silent; but when he became too unreasonable, I could not contain myself and I told dear Mr. Matthews quite plainly that I was fully convinced that God endowed the blacks with the same mental resources as the whites, and that in a better life he should not expect to find such caste and color distinctions as there are here.

"I like much of what I have read of 'Uncle Tom's Cabin'; the manners and the speech of the Negroes and also of the planters are faithfully depicted. It seems to me as if it would be difficult to translate, for the Negroes speak very badly and their speech is impossible for anyone who has not been in their midst to understand. However, I have, thank God, not seen any such planters like a couple of them described there nor witnessed the least mistreatment; on the contrary, they are treated more humanely and are more outspoken than white servants at home. All the Negroes

2 J. H. Matthews of Georgia (Mrs. Laurell's note).

groes have their own chickens and pigs, which they sell as they choose; they have required work to do during the day, and when they have finished that, as sometimes happens as early as 12 o'clock, they may work for themselves. The female servant who nurses and looks after the children is called their Mauma; Anna has received from her Mauma a silver mug, quite beautiful, and gold cuff links. You should see the little black waiters, William and Ben, 8 and 6 years old, and their two-year-old little brother Pin playing on the piazza and also in the parlor with little Anna, and you would be amazed to see the intimacy with which the black and white children's heads lean together in their play. It cannot be denied that slavery can give rise to misfortunes and appalling behavior, but in general it is far, far better than we are able to conceive. They also seem satisfied and happy, are especially devoted to their master and mistress, and often lead a more carefree life than they. If any of them become sick, they immediately receive medication and sympathetic care until they have completely recovered. The tenant farmers on many estates in Sweden are far unhappier than slaves on many plantations and are more likely to be mistreated, indeed to be more enslaved than the former. I have not seen the slightest mistreatment of a Negro." In a letter of 26 April 1853 to her mother, Rosalie added: "The slave owners have, you see, far more interest in them than our landed proprietors have in their tenantry, and it is just this self-interest that provides a powerful reason for treating them well even if moral reasons are lacking."

When Rosalie had finished reading Mrs. Stowe's book, she returned to the subject of its accuracy in a letter to her father dated 3 June 1853: "'Uncle Tom's Cabin' is really very well written and in my view well intentioned, although I trust she has made use of rather flamboyant colors. . . . Most 'Southerners' are up in arms against Mrs. Stowe; many do not want to read her book in order to avoid being angered by it; others read and condemn or ridicule it, and a few try to do justice to the author's talents and character. Among these few is Eliza, who with the fire and passion of youth for everything noble and beautiful would gladly abolish slavery if she could. Dr. Matthews belongs to the other class; when he was last here, he said that he was really indignant with Mrs. Stowe for the reception she had got in England, besides trying in every way to disparage her.

"The most frequent argument is that the poor people in the northern states are much worse off than are the Negroes; another is that the blacks there have a worse time of it than here since a greater prejudice against them prevails there and white servants are preferred. Dr. Matthews had brought with him a book entitled 'Northern and Southern Slavery,'[3] intended to counteract Uncle Tom. If I had time I would like to translate a book that I am now reading, 'Recollections of a Southern Matron'[4] by a lady from Connecticut now residing in Charleston, Mrs. Gilman; this narrative is simple and unaffected and contains a faithful description of the way of life and customs on the plantations.

"We have for that matter an Uncle Tom here, Daddy Jimmie, whom all the members of the family are devoted to and place great trust in." Rosalie wrote also to Hedda Hammarsköld, 8 May 1853, about the controversial book: "My conviction is the same as it has always been, that God did not create certain races of people to be the work horses for others, that such a relationship is unnatural and odious and that sooner or later it will be dissolved although not without hard fighting. Where the master is a good and noble person, the fate of his slaves is perhaps to be preferred to the majority of white servants—but everything depends on that if."

As early as 1 April Rosalie was writing her mother about the oppressively warm and humid weather which had kept her from performing her duties efficiently and had obliged her to spend all her free time putting her summer dresses in order. She had much to report about the domestic manners of the Peronneaus: "What I missed in the beginning was bread, which is never used except when rolls are sometimes brought home from the city. Rice, hominy, waffles, and pancakes substitute for bread. Breakfast consists of coffee and tea, a main dish (fish, ham, or sausage), hominy, waffles, pancakes, and butter. Dinner of pea soup (make from a kind of brown pea, resembling our 'bruna bönor'), followed by two or three meat dishes and sometimes fish, rice, and hominy, occasionally corncakes. One dish is set before the master, one before the mistress, and both ask, 'May I serve you some of this dish,' 'Would you care for a piece of chicken,' 'Which

3 Unidentified proslavery tract, evidently one of many then being published under similar titles and contrasting slavery in the South favorably with the abuse or neglect of free Negroes in the North.

4 A sentimental romance (New York, 1838) by Caroline Gilman, whose husband was a Unitarian minister serving at Charleston. The narrative, cast in the form of memoirs, of Cornelia Wilton's coming of age on a plantation located near Charleston allows her to display the full range of her sensibility in response to episodes of unrequited love, careless flirtation, infant death, and so on. Her piety is perhaps no more cloyingly shown than in her refusing to sing a popular air on a Sunday (pp. 72–73), an apposite demonstration to Rosalie of a "southern" attitude deplored in her letters. Cornelia's refusal to desecrate the Sabbath was reenacted even more passionately by little Elsie Dinsmore in a famous episode in the 1868 novel by Martha Finley.

piece would you prefer," etc.[5] Usually there is some kind of poultry on the table although there has been a shortage for some time, roast and stewed chicken, ham, roast beef, pork, lamb, venison, but always two or three sorts. When we have dessert it consists usually of rice pudding or cake and custard. The table is then cleared before the dessert is brought in. We sit at the table for a long time, usually an hour. The service is provided by an old retainer, Daddy Jimmie, reared in the Peronneau family which he would never want to abandon; he reads and writes and occasionally serves as the priest for the other Negroes; an old woman, Mauma Tina, keeps the peacock feathers in motion to chase away the flies; three small boys, Pal, Ben, and William, 9, 7, and 5 years old, who are quite agile, come running with their trays. Supper, which consists of tea and coffee, waffles or pancakes or some sort of cakes, is brought into the parlor where we all assemble in the evenings. Clean napkins are supplied every day, also hand towels."

At this time Rosalie was also writing her father, 4 April 1853, about the number of guests the Peronneaus had had. Relatives from Charleston and Georgia had been visiting the family, and also young Dr. Samuel Logan, from whose father Peronneau was renting "Dungannon." The gentlemen amused themselves hunting, and in the evenings there were music and dancing. "Saturday was a real work day, for in order to satisfy everybody's wishes, I had to set up tableaux, difficult enough in themselves since I did not have the prerequisites but had myself to contrive and assemble everything that was needed. It was killingly hot also, 86° F (30° C), so I was tired out when it was over. However, it succeeded beyond expectation, and they were loud in their approval. Dr. de Saussure, young Dr. Peronneau's brother-in-law, had never before seen tableaux vivants and declared that I had 'immortalized myself'! Five were taken from 'Hamlet' and in one of them we also had the ghost. Mr. Parker was a splendid Hamlet. The last tableau represented a gypsy scene and also came off well. Then we danced a little. Sunday was spent reading, conversing, and promenading."

Rosalie's mother evidently had expressed a certain degree of anxiety that Rosalie would find a spouse amid all the agreeable company she was

---

5 In an amusing account of her visit to Macon, Georgia, Fredrika Bremer also wrote of the unceasing concern of her host, hostess, and servants for her welfare, in her case because she had taken no pickles on her plate—"pickle persecution" she called it and thereby gave additional cause for the many complaints of southern readers of her ingratitude for their hospitality. *Homes of the New World* (London and New York, 1853), 1, 335–36.

keeping and would wish to remain in America for good, but she received a reassuring answer, 31 March 1853: "We are not to give thought to any alteration in my circumstances—such fancies have long ago flown out of my sight; it was not God's will that such would be my lot in life, and you will have to satisfy yourselves seeing your Rosa among the poor despised and derided old maids. I fear, however, that I will not become so sweetly good-natured an old mamsell as Aunt Fredrika in the feuilleton, who was ready to help everybody, you remember, and died with her apron on. But I mean to do my best not to become one of those who live only for themselves and seem to be completely worthless members of society. Even a single woman can find a pleasant and useful round of activity if she looks for it, and although she cannot be rewarded as is a wife and mother for her solicitude, she can nevertheless in her own consciousness discover her reward and consolation for the sneers of thoughtless people. . . . Once I am home again, I shall have to make plans to earn my livelihood in some fashion, for I am now too accustomed to and satisfied with pecuniary independence to be able to endure the opposite. I hope then that I may with some certainty be able to give instruction in English, which I now speak completely free of difficulty." She continued the subject in her letter of 4 April to her father: "When I come home and can feel more independent then than I did before, I intend not to frequent other society than that which pleases me and to which I can give pleasure, and above all no large supés, which along with the duty visits that go with them arouse in me a kind of horror. . . . However much I like America and am truly attached to several of its inhabitants, it would be impossible for me to harbor the thought of staying here forever. It seems to me as though my heart would always feel itself to be a stranger, as though a wall, even if only of glass, were to stand between me and them. No, no, no, I must come home, for I could not ever feel happy in the long run elsewhere. The thought of parents and brothers and sisters would always cast a shadow over the happiest moments. Besides, I would not want to own slaves."

In another of her general letters to "all my dear ones," Rosalie added details on 1 May 1853 to her descriptions of life in her new home. "We were out a while ago to the rice fields and saw a recently killed alligator, about two ells long. They are indeed dreadfully ugly. When we were coming home from church a couple of weeks ago, two of them appeared, even larger, on the banks of a stream which we were crossing. They seemed completely motionless, sunk in a deep torpor, but when our driver jumped down from the carriage to frighten them, they dived down into the water immediately. They are the same color as the muddy river, so that at first I could not distinguish them from it. They take sheep and goats when they possibly can, and instances are cited of their even having taken children. Dr. Logan told me about a Negro woman working in a rice field who had set down her small child under a tree; alarmed by the child's screams she hurried to the place but arrived only in time to see an alligator diving with the child. Such events, however, are as seldom here as the attacks on people by wolves at home. I have not yet seen a rattlesnake, but a couple of long black snakes which are said to be harmless; and also a copperhead, with markings like the squares on a chessboard, really beautiful. It was dead when I saw it; otherwise I probably would not have examined it so carefully. A Negro girl on one of the neighboring plantations had been bitten the other day by a poisonous spider, and with such serious consequences that there was concern for her life. But through appropriate treatment she was saved. For poisonous bites spirits are used here as medicine. . . .

"Some weeks ago we had a special sort of drama here. The so-called reserve, a sort of little pond or pool, had been drained, for the rice fields were to be placed under water. Mr. Peronneau and a number of the Negroes went down to fish, and we to look on. At the bottom of the dried out reserve, heaps of fish were lying, and in one little pool and stream next to it the water was scarcely visible because of the fish. They threw out nets which were filled instantly and raked up fish in heaps; they filled up baskets with them, and everywhere on the grass the poor creatures flapped about, so hastily removed from their natural element."

Rosalie wrote also to her father on 1 May from "Dungannon": "Soon we shall have to leave since it becomes more dangerous every day to stay here. It is especially the evening air which is so injurious, and therefore we must not be outdoors late. This is indeed a peculiar climate with its strongly marked variations within short distances. All the planters are beginning now to get ready to move, some to the city, others to the Pineland.[6] The girls give me a not very tempting description of the latter

6 F. A. Porcher's memoirs (see p. 36, n. 3, above) include a description of this region that parallels Rosalie's observations here and later: "There is something in the Pineland of our Low Country which has nothing like it in any other part of the world, everything is strange; there is the forest, but it suggests no ideas of gloom; there are the smiling blossoms of Spring and Summer but they have none of the gladness which they create elsewhere. Your forest is so bare of underwood that your vision is scarcely bounded by the branchless trees; and the jealous care of preserving the healthfulness of the place induced the people to interdict all cultivation of the soil, so that neither fruit nor flower garden could be enjoyed. It is so natural, when we find ourselves in possession of even a rood of land, to turn some of it to account either for profit or for pleasure that this stern abnegation of enjoyment is one of the most striking features of a pineland residence." "The Memoirs . . . ," *South Carolina Historical and Genealogical Magazine* 45 (1944), 30.

place, which consists of great pine forests so dense and tall that the sky can scarcely be seen. But many flowers are said to grow there, and that will help console me. Also moving are a neighboring family, the Fishburns, whose two daughters were at Limestone last year, and young Dr. Logan, who has his practice in this and in the adjoining parishes." Before long, 30 May 1853, Rosalie was writing from "Bentwood," the Peronneaus' summer home in the Pineland, a letter addressed to "all my beloved": "I suppose that you are curious to hear something of our new residence, to which we moved the 15th of May. The whole week before, we—and especially Mrs. Peronneau—were occupied with sorting out the things which should be taken, packing, and so on. They did not want me to go there until everything was ready. Eliza, who does not like the Pineland at all, was very much concerned that I would find it too dreary. The girls and little Anna set out in the morning. In the afternoon the rest of the company got under way, the undersigned on horseback, escorted by Mr. Ned Parker, and had a very delightful ride. I rode on a little pony with the euphonious name of Hamlet, and as he rode remarkably well, it was a real pleasure. I sit sidesaddle firmly now, an incomparably pleasanter way to ride. On the way we made a little detour to a huge mulberry tree and a stand of plum trees and therefore did not arrive until the others had been here a while. Mrs. Peronneau came to welcome me and then showed me to my room, where all my things were already set out, and flowers from 'Dungannon' greeted me. . . .

"How can so short a distance produce so much difference in climate and healthfulness? It is, however, an indisputable fact. With the coming of the month of May the plantations in the Low Country begin to be regarded as dangerous. We were not to go outdoors after sunset, nor to be up and about too early while the ground still shimmered with the morning dew. It was strange to see the difference in vegetation in the course of our approaching the Pineland. When we drove away from 'Dungannon' on the highway, trees and vines formed dense walls on both sides, and here and there overhanging trees and vines arched over the road, a perfect luxuriance of fresh greenery in many variations. About one and a half miles from 'Dungannon' we turned off onto the Pineland road. Out there dark pines rose up among the still numerous shade trees, but the underbrush was still dense and abundant vines adorned trees and bushes. After a while the pines began to take exclusive possession, the brush became thinner and more meager, the vines almost nonexistent—we were in the Pineland, where the ground was, however, alive and green with small shrubs, ferns, very beautiful blueberries (not like ours but big bushes), and flowers. The live oaks, however, had completely vanished, and the festoons of moss no longer adorned the trees. . . .

"The reason the Pineland is so much more healthful than the plantations has been told me as follows: When the great bogs and ponds have been thoroughly warmed up by the strong sun, and the surrounding land also, injurious vapors rise up during the night from them which cause shivering and fevers, especially so-called 'country fever.' This is not the case in the Pineland, where first of all the land is somewhat higher and drier, and second, the trees there stand so close to one another that the sun cannot have the same effect as it does in open places. Also the nights here are always cool. Right within the woods there are some houses, for the most part log houses, to which the planters must come with their families as a refuge in the summer. These dwellings are extremely simple and recall the dwellings of the first colonists in the virgin forests. Although ours is very plain, it has nevertheless an advantage over the others I have seen, for it is built of boards and is whitewashed. At the top of a long flight of stairs there is a piazza which extends along the length of the parlor, the bedroom, and one of the girls' rooms. Under Eliza's room there is the storeroom; under mine, a little room which is now occupied by Dr. Logan. The other part of the building is still open underneath, but there is talk of locating a schoolroom there, which is indeed needed, for now we have nothing other than the parlor, which is rather awkward when company comes. The walls and ceiling consist of rough boards with beams between, whitewashed. In my opinion, my room is the most pleasant, but it is a perfect lantern, for though not larger than my room at home it has five windows. Outside two of the windows I have shelves containing flowers which Mrs. Peronneau had had sent up from the garden at 'Dungannon.'"

Young Dr. Logan was now of course even more in evidence than he had been at "Dungannon." "He is going on twenty-two years and has just begun to practice, and the Peronneau family has invited him to live here until he has had time to repair his Pineland house. He is very agreeable and unaffected, nearly always brings some flowers home for me. The other day I was given a beautiful bunch of gardenias, extraordinarily fragrant." Rosalie described in detail these and other flowers which had enchanted her, and when the perfume of some was so strong as to give her a headache, Mr. Peronneau became alarmed by her flower worship. "One fine day we shall no doubt go to Miss Roos's room and find her half dead from having had so many flowers all about. This will never do, for I am responsible for her!—They all think of me as soon as they lay eyes on a new flower." Rosalie's love of nature was acknowledged not only with flowers. One day Mr. Peronneau shot a redbird and since it had fallen into a thorny thicket and was difficult to bring in, he asked in recompense to have two extra pieces on the piano after dinner. He loved to hear Swedish folk melodies; "Näckens polska" was a favorite, and Rosalie wrote home for more music. For her part, she sent stuffed birds and birds' eggs to her brother-in-law the forester, as well as seeds of which a part was to be forwarded to Professor Elias Fries in Uppsala. She sent tomato seed to be used at "Sjögerås," but it would be more than fifty years before tomatoes would be grown in quantity in Sweden. The forester sent in return stuffed Swedish birds, including a great horned owl, which were donated to the newly opened Museum in Charleston. "Not far from here and visible among the trees are some houses belonging to the Logan family, who also own 'Berry Hill' and 'Dungannon.' In former times they lived at the latter place, and the Peronneaus at 'Berry Hill' directly opposite. In summer both families moved to their Pineland residences. The Logan family, which besides the mother and father consisted of 14 children, must have been agreeable and pleasant, to judge by what I have seen of them. . . . The mother [Anna Glover Logan] died three years ago, and the father sold off what he could of his property and made his way with his children and Negroes to Louisiana where one of his brothers lives, and there he bought a sugar plantation. Before he got his own house ready, he lived with his brother, and from there he wanted to take his family with him by boat on the Mississippi to their new home. He would not be dissuaded from this resolve although his brother pleaded with him; all that he succeeded in doing was to take two of the girls, who were already down at the boat, and send them instead by carriage to their new dwelling. Mr. Logan with his three sons and five Negroes traveled by boat, and all went well until they were near the place where they intended to go ashore. Then the current drove a huge timber raft against them which turned the boat over, and everyone except Mr. Logan himself and one of the boys perished in the waves. . . . Misfortune dogged Logan still further; several of his Negroes died, and in a flood the banks of his plantation along the river as well as several sugar fields were destroyed so that he felt himself obliged to sell it. He returned last year with the remainder of his family and has now moved to Charleston to find means there of providing for himself and his family. Although he still has his plantations, he has no benefit from them, for the rice fields are blocked up and he lacks means and the help to bring them back into cultivation and to rebuild the deteriorating cabins of the Negroes.

"Several such abandoned plantations with burned down houses and blocked up fields and gardens lie round about. You see, the first rice plantations were laid out around the great marshes or bogs in the Low Country, but then they discovered that rice could be cultivated to greater profit on the river banks where the water supply was plentiful, and so they abandoned those places. Therefore there are in this community vast extents which no one owns or for which the owners have shown not the slightest concern. We took a walk once from 'Dungannon' to such a place where the dwelling house had been burned down (a favorite sport of the poor people around here!), so that only the chimneys remained. There were one or two fruit trees here and there; the burial grounds (every plantation has such) were overgrown with trees and bushes. . . . Mr. Peronneau's plantation, 'Standyard,' was also one of these abandoned places so that he bought it at a good price but at the same time has had to expend an incredible amount of labor upon it. He rides out there every morning after breakfast and does not return until 6 or 7 in the evening, without having partaken of any food in all that time. The first years he had it, he is said to have gone out there even earlier in the morning and not come home until 10 or 11 at night. He would not have been able to endure it without tobacco, he says, and indeed he does use it copiously." Mr. Peronneau had also recently purchased an abandoned plantation adjacent to "Standyard" in order to ensure a good water supply. Its abundance of plums and mulberries lured the family to pleasant excursions there, and Rosalie was promised a cottage in the midst of that splendor if she agreed to stay or to come back. All about in the fields she saw huge, dead live oaks standing, killed by their former owners: "So that the trees would not shade the fields, a deep ring had been chopped around the trunk so that they would die. To chop down these giants would have required too much work. Then the ground was hoed a little for the planting of corn."

From the Pineland she wrote her father, 3 June 1853: "Dearest Papa, I have surely the best reasons in the world to be grateful to God for His goodness, for especially since I have been in America it seems to me almost as though I were under His immediate protection. How lonely and depressed I felt when the first stretch of the American coastline came into view! It was then that I understood for the first time the extent of the step I had taken, and my courage faltered, but only for a moment. I fled to the Almighty and All-Good in devout prayer. I confided myself trustingly to His care, and my faith has not been disappointed. . . . You indicate that you were surprised when I did not give up my plans to travel despite my having been thrown on my own when the priest's family had to stay behind. But that proves that you do not know your Rosa, for when I have reached a decision or determined upon a goal, the fulfillment or the gaining of which depends on strength of will and perseverance, I do not shrink from the difficulties, they do not cause me to falter or to grow weary—no, they only egg me on. There is something in me of 'la vieille garde meurt mais ne se donne pas.'[7] I admit that I played for fairly high stakes and might have had to endure suffering and trials of which I had not the least notion at home, but as it has turned out, I couldn't be happier at having persisted in my decision.

"I too was surprised, surprised that you and Mama let me go, something that I, in all candor, did not suppose possible, and that I in the same position would never have been able to allow myself to do, for it just as easily could have ended unhappily for me as it has for many others. However, I shall always be grateful for your consent and support, which has had the most beneficial consequences for me. The goodness and the friendship which have been shown me on all sides cannot be valued too highly."

Rosalie was given a vacation for the month of July and together with Hulda Hahr accepted the invitation of Carl Hammarsköld's family to visit them in their new home in Spring Hill, North Carolina.[8] Because she would be traveling alone on the first stage of the journey to Orangeburg, her friends arranged that she would have suitable escort, in this case Dr. John Bachman, pastor of St. John's Lutheran church in Charleston.[9] In a letter dated 19 June 1853 to her brother-in-law Rosalie wrote: "Our conversation proceeded almost without interruption although it was rather taxing because of the clatter caused by the cars. We talked mostly about flowers and travel; he is a keen botanist and has traveled throughout a large part of Europe. He exhorted me also not to lapse from my religion and urged me to come to his church when I am in Charleston, for I would always find a place in his pew." There was a short wait at Orangeburg, and Rosalie took the opportunity to become acquainted with Hulda Hahr's school and its headmaster, the Reverend Legaré. The visit became a subject for one of her letters, 11 August 1853, to "all my dear ones." "The school is not in such a grand style as Limestone; there are only 30

7 "The old guard dies but does not submit."

8 At iron works located by Rosalie 33 miles northeast of Limestone Springs, probably in Gaston County.

9 Collaborator with J. J. Audubon on *The Viviparous Quadrupeds of North America* (1845–48) and Professor of Natural History in the College of Charleston. F. A. Porcher's memoirs (see p. 85, n. 6) may again be allowed to supplement Rosalie's report. Bachman was not only one of the most eminent members of The Conversation Club in Charleston, Porcher wrote, but also one of the most amiable. "He had a very tolerant spirit for every thing except spirits, both material and moral, and against anyone who doubted the unity of the human race." "The Memoirs. . . .," *South Carolina Historical and Genealogical Magazine* 47 (1947), 218. Also see Preface, p. xii.

full-time boarders, and it is all run on a more familiar, intimate footing, whereas at Limestone more emphasis is placed on etiquette and discipline. . . . Hulda is greatly admired at Orangeburg and Mr. Legaré would not give her up for anything. He said he did not intend to be 'such a goose' as Mr. Curtis." Mr. Legaré's son, "a handsome, likeable young man," made himself agreeable to Hulda both in and out of school. (She married him in 1862; her brother Franz also married and remained in America.) Rosalie's letter continues: "Mr. Fitch, a young gentleman of Mr. Legaré's acquaintance, was commissioned to escort us to Columbia. We had great fun on the way eating peaches and ice cream which are served in the summer on the larger railroads. It was hot and dusty, and after we arrived at Columbia we had to work hard to get clean again before we could go out. Our young protector invited us to his parents' home for supper; they also welcomed us with the greatest cordiality, took our mantillas and hats and looked out some fans for us. The father, a doctor, not especially old but blind, enjoyed very much hearing about our strange, distant country. . . . I relate these events as evidence of the natives' hospitality toward strangers.

"The next day, Mr. Fitch came and conveyed us and our baggage to the cars for Chester, and since Carl Hammarsköld met us at Chester after we had found a protector in Mr. Warren on the way, we were free of any sort of 'trouble' during the journey. After having become used to the flat, broad roads in the Low Country, these up here seemed worse than ever; there isn't a moment's rest while traveling, for one is tossed back and forth in all directions."

Rosalie remarked on the relative primitiveness of life in these parts, still close to pioneering days. There was much speculation in iron ore, and rumors of the discovery of gold[10] in the mountains or streams aroused great expectations: "They imagine they see gold everywhere, and almost insane purchases are contracted for." Hammarsköld too had high hopes and attached great importance to the detection of any gold, however meager. Perhaps it held forth for him the possibility of paying off debts and returning honorably to his home country. But he preferred not to talk about Sweden; "we would be better off to forget it," he said. Both the father and son were working hard, but they had yet to make their fortune. A fresh disaster was to strike the family at the end of the summer when a torrential flood swept away both the smithy and the saw at Spring Hill.

---

10 Gold had been discovered near King's Mountain, not far from Hammarsköld's works, in 1829; up to 1840 $60,000 worth had been taken out. North Carolina and Georgia were the leading gold-mining states until the discovery of gold in California in 1848.

Once during the several weeks Rosalie and Hulda spent with the Hammarskölds, they made a brief excursion to Limestone. As usual, the road there, a distance of thirty-three miles, presented many difficulties and unexpected obstacles, in part because of recent heavy rains. "All of a sudden Carl drives against a stump in the middle of the road with the result that the piece [whiffletree] to which the traces are fastened behind the horse broke right in two. There was no one living closer than 1 mile away, and Carl had to unhitch one of the horses to ride for help. There we were, Hulda and I, alone in the middle of the forest after sunset. I felt no fear, however, but jumped down to hold the horse by the bridle. After a long while Carl returned with a Negro carrying an axe, and a little tree now had to relinquish its trunk in order to repair the damage. . . . Exhausted beyond all description we finally reached Limestone close to 10 o'clock. Everything was still and silent in the seminary, but from the hotel, which was lighted up, could be heard the tones of a violin and sounds of dancing. We felt little inclined to join them there, however, and Carl went to stay with Franz, who had not yet gone to bed, and we were taken in hand by Miss Wilson." In the morning they received an unmistakably warm reception: "We were immediately surrounded now, embraced and kissed, before we even had time to distinguish by whom. . . . They overwhelmed us with pleas to stay several days, but we had to decline since Carl had to be back home the following day. They had just been having examinations. The graduating class had written on <u>Addison</u>, the next one on the <u>Age of Pericles</u>. But the awards were based not only on the best composition but also on the best grades. In the evening the prize essays were read aloud and awarded gold and silver medals.

"After this there was a concert; the instrumental music was good. The overture to 'The Barber' was played in an arrangement for four pianos, but the vocal music was weak.

"The next morning we awoke to a downpour, rather discouraging. Several of the girls who had concluded their studies were called for by their relatives; others went home for a visit to rest up after the examination frenzy. Carriage after carriage rolled up and started off, trunks were carried down, farewells exchanged, and Limestone little by little began to lose the happy, festive appearance that had distinguished it for several days.

"When around 11 o'clock the rain held up a bit, we started out on the return journey but now took a different road and were back at the Hammarskölds' by 11 o'clock in the evening."

There they were astonished to find Mr. Legaré waiting for them on his way home from New York and now hoping to act as the young ladies' escort on the journey back to Orangeburg. They met with no unexpected difficulties on the return trip, but it was a little annoying to be obliged to wait until 1 a.m. on Monday after staying in Winnsboro because it would not do to travel on a Sunday. Rosalie wished she could share with her family in Sweden the marvelous peaches that friendly fellow travelers offered them on the way. She received a heart-warming welcome on her return to the Pineland: new curtains in her room, fresh flowers in the vases, on her bureau peaches on a beautiful porcelain plate, and a row of gifts from each of the children "with love." "On my shelves lay three dozen new hand towels marked Rosalie Roos. How kind they truly are to me!"

VIII

LIFE IN CHARLESTON

Writing from the Pineland to her mother 29 September 1853, Rosalie was once again moved to report on weather such as she had never known in Sweden: "It rains and thunders here nearly every day with the disagreeable consequence that everything gets mildewed: books, clothes, shoes, but almost worst of all, my flowers, with which I have taken such pains. Mr. Peronneau borrowed for me a very complete 'Flora' from the library in Charleston, and I was about to begin laying my flowers in the herbarium when to my great distress I see that they are completely mildewed. I dried them off one Saturday but on the following they looked just as bad again and I was almost ready to leave them to their fate but could not quite bring myself to it since I have probably more than 300 specimens.

"The other day we had a little adventure. We were out riding one morning before breakfast with Dr. Logan as the chauffeur. The road in the Pineland is very narrow so that whoever is driving has to keep his eyes peeled to avoid hitting trees or the stumps which line the road. On the way back Dr. Logan drove into a stump hidden in the high grass with such speed that the carriage was thrown on its side, Dr. Logan and Mary were thrown off, and Jimmie hung on outside upside down. It all happened so quickly. Clelia and I, who were sitting inside, got nothing worse than a good shaking up and a fright. Dr. Logan had been deafened by the impact and at first could not speak; the horses ran away with the wagon tongue that had broken off, and I after them shouting 'whoa' as soon as I saw that no one had been injured. They stopped readily enough so that I had hold of them before Dr. Logan reached the place. Fortunately, no serious damage was done . . . and after we had picked up the pieces scattered about, we strolled home (2 miles) and found everybody perfectly calm since they had been informed of the accident by Miss Logan and Henry, who were on horseback."

To her father the next month, 24 October 1853, Rosalie reported details of the economics of living in Charleston: "I happened to be in Charleston when your last letter came, and I passed on to Emilie questions you had asked about the cost of living in Charleston. Their small house, which when they bought it contained five small rooms and a piazza with appurtenant outhouses, kitchen, and servants' quarters, as well as two small gardens, cost $3000 but is not situated on one of the most desirable streets. It is much better to buy one's home than to rent, for rents are very high; a house like the Hammarskölds' would cost $300 to $350, and less than a house cannot be rented since every family occupies his own. Emilie estimated that all the expenses for a family of four would come to 3 or 4 thousand dollars using black servants, who are regarded as being more suitable than white. Any agreements with white servants are not binding, for they simply go their way without their employer's being able to get them back solely through the power of persuasion. As soon as they have been in America for a time, they absorb distorted notions about freedom and equality and regard all menial tasks as being beneath them, which foolish arrogance continues until need convinces them of their error. The Hammarskölds in North Carolina have acquired a horror of white servants, so much have they suffered from those whom they brought over with them and who caused them countless vexations and finally ran off, with all but a couple of exceptions. The blacks, however, are less efficient than the whites, and according to Mr. Peronneau one can count two blacks for one white."

On the last pages of one of Rosalie's notebooks there is a list of market prices in Charleston on 17 February 1855 written in another hand presumably at Rosalie's request so that she might provide her father with correct information on her return home:

Negroes	Men	800	to	1,200	dollars
	Women	600	to	1,000	"
	Children	200	to	600	"
Horses		50	"	150	"
Mules		50	"	150	"
Cows		8	"	25	"
Sheep		1	"	2	"
Chickens		8	"	12	cents
Eggs, doz.		6	"	10	"
Turkey		37	"	62	"
Ducks		12½			"
Geese		37½			"

Rosalie's father clearly wanted to have exact information about life in the America of his dreams. In Rosalie's letter of 24 October he was given answers to many questions he had asked concerning which trees and bushes grew in the region, which berries, cultivated and wild, which kinds of crops were grown, and so on. "Fences here usually are set in a zigzag such as I pictured in my drawing of Limestone. It is called a Virginia fence or worm fence. I have also seen fences with heavy steel wire attached to poles. I really know nothing about the implements though I know plows are used.

"Milk is not used in food except occasionally in puddings and custards; otherwise only for coffee and tea, for which cream is not used. The coffee is boiled here with milk, which is quite good. The cows are driven home at evening to be milked, again in the morning. The calves are not allowed to feed themselves, and at some places the calves are kept in a pen during the day so that the mothers will return to them by themselves; at night the cows change places with the calves and the latter are allowed out. Butter is churned here in the summer for household needs, but in the winter northern butter is purchased."

Mr. Peronneau took Rosalie along to the rice fields and gave her a great deal of information about cultivation and harvesting which she passed on in a letter 16 November 1853 to "all my dear ones": "In good years the harvest can go as high as 60 bushels an acre, but ordinarily the yield is 40 to 50 bushels an acre, and in that case each hand will be credited with $270, that is, every full-grown worker earns that amount for his master. Instances can be cited when an acre yielded up to 74 bushels, but that, however, is very rare.

"I asked Mr. Peronneau how much capital is needed to become a rice planter, and he replied that if he had to buy all his laborers, about $20,000 would be needed for that, and $10,000 to $20,000 for the land. If there is a good supply of water, rice cultivation is fairly easy, if only the fields are left in peace by airborne marauders, a kind of small bird called rice birds, which come in great flocks a little before the rice ripens and do unbelievable damage; Mr. Peronneau reckons the damage they do to him at 400 or 500 bushels. They come in enormous flocks and remain in a rice field as long as there is anything to be had. They are slightly larger than an Ortolan sparrow and are eaten as a great delicacy. Some days Mr. Peronneau had as many as five men shooting these birds, and thousands of them were killed. When they fly up into the air, the flock is so large and numerous that it resembles a huge black cloud. Once when I was there, Mr. Peronneau sent a Negro to scare them so that I might see this. Every day for a fortnight if not longer we had rice birds for breakfast, dinner, and the evening meal. There were days, surely, when more than one hundred were consumed. A great many are also sent to friends and acquaintances in town. It is scarcely worth my trying to describe how fat they were, you would doubt my word, and that would be too bad. They are fried in their own fat and seem to swim in grease lying on the plate."

As the summer drew to a close, Rosalie had much to relate to her brother Emil, 27 October 1853: "Our stay in the Pineland is coming to an end, and we begin to think of moving back to the plantation, for with the coming of autumn and cold weather we shall be out of danger from its unhealthfulness. We have been here for more than five months, but however much the girls feared for it, this period has seemed not at all unpleasant to me, for I have always had my time taken up with things to do.

"There is yet another family living near here, the Fishburns, who have 11 children. Our contacts during the summer have been limited to just a few visits, but since the cooler weather has arrived and the Fishburns have finished adding on a large room, we have been together several times, and remarkably enough for America, the dancing was quite smart. Mrs. Fishburn is cheerful and pleasant, a good hostess who wants the young people to enjoy themselves and is indefatigable in playing for them. She looks quite young still although she has four full-grown children, three very beautiful daughters and a son who also is good-looking. The dancers are in addition made up of a younger daughter and a son, and we have four daughters in addition to the undersigned, and Dr. Logan, at times even Henry, so you see we have a rather full complement. I have taught them several of our dances like the cotillion, the clap anglaise, the mill dance, the curtsey dance and polska, all of which please them mightily, and they are of one mind that Sweden must be a most delightful country. It really gave me pleasure to see them dancing our old faithful polska, for which they succeeded in getting even the old folks on their feet, and they all danced with the same vigor and merriment as in the old days at dear 'Sjögerås.' Even your beloved sister, 'she who would never dance again,' had to participate in the dance and was in fact much in demand, and what is more, I still am in high spirits and delighted by it. For the waltz, schottische (do they dance it at home?) and the polska, it does not do here for the gentlemen to hold the ladies by the waist; that would be considered an horreur, but the way he leads his lady is to hold both her hands crosswise, her right one in his right, and her left in his left. Even with this modification there is very little dancing of waltzes, polskas, and schottisches at public balls. . . .

"We have also had a wedding here. In the Pineland live several poor families called Crackers who sometimes have a small piece of land which they cultivate, sometimes a small herd which yields enough to feed them and which one sometimes sees them herding together riding with long whips in their hands. One of these who lives two miles from here has a small field, some cows, and peach trees bearing sweet fruit. A rumor quickly spread that his eldest daughter Mary, a sturdy, plump, hard-working girl, was engaged to a Dutchman (so are nearly all foreigners called, at least Germans, by the lower class). When asked, her brother at first would admit to nothing, but finally the truth came out. The girls saw to the bride's and her sister's toilet, and we received written invitations to the wedding. As it took place shortly after our upset, when the wagon tongue was broken, we had no carriage, but a large wagon was filled with rugs and pillows, and so off we went, eight girls strong, for on the way to the bride's house we had stopped to call for the Fishburn girls. The bride wore a white cambric dress, a white sash, and a veil on her head. The assemblage was large, consisting of nearly all the inhabitants of the Pineland, dressed up in their best, but they looked as serious and solemn as though they had been to a funeral. Four or five babies completed the congregation. They begged Anna Peronneau and me, who were dressed in white, to officiate as bridesmaids, and of course we consented. The priest was Presbyterian and began the ceremony by asking if anyone present had objections to the marriage to speak now or forever hold his peace. And then with his eyes closed he said a couple of extemporaneous prayers and joined their hands—and so it was done. Congratulations followed, and after that, cakes and wine. We then drove home, for Mr. Peronneau did not want to let us be out late on the roads, but the gentlemen went back in the evening and partook of a supper which was served at the farm and was abundant, and joined in the dance which continued the whole night."

At the end of October the Peronneau family was back at "Dungannon," and the workday resumed its usual course, but for the older girls the possibility loomed of their being allowed to attend the big event of the autumn in Charleston, a regatta launched at the end of November. Sure enough, an invitation came to the whole family from close relatives. The girls exerted all their persuasive powers to have their parents fall in with their plans. To her mother Rosalie wrote, 2 December 1853: "After a certain amount of 'grumbling,' about horses and so on, Mr. Peronneau finally gave in, and it was decided that Mrs. Peronneau, who leaves her home so seldom and so reluctantly, should also go along in order to visit her sisters in the city. She cannot leave the boys and little Anna at home, so that it became a pilgrimage for the entire family. The girls left yesterday, and today we shall follow, but as usually happens when there are many who are to travel, including a number of children, the sun had already begun to set when we started out." When they reached the landing at the Ashley, they learned that the last ferry had already left and that there was no possibility of crossing that evening. What was to be done? Relatives lived on a plantation fairly close by, but the children there had come down with whooping cough. It was decided then to call at another plantation owned by a bachelor who was said to be away from home. "It was already dark when we got there and took the servants in the house by surprise with the arrival of a barouche, a buggy, and a cart filled with baggage. Mr. Peronneau, who was known to them, explained the circumstances and said that they must give us house room for the night, to which they assented with alacrity, regretting only that they did not have things in as good order as they would have liked." The company settled down in the parlor and while waiting for a cup of tea, Rosalie had time to look about and to use the evening for writing letters: "This dwelling seems to fulfill the ideas I used to entertain of comfortable bachelor's quarters whose owner has a refined and cultured taste and the means to satisfy it. . . . The floor is covered with a beautiful rug, and the furniture consists of a divan covered with Turkish tapestry, several beautiful armchairs in cane, one of them a most comfortable easy chair, as well as other comfortable armchairs, bookcases, a cabinet for curios, and some tables.

"On a sideboard are some superb bowls of real Chinese porcelain; over the sofa hang pipes and a dagger from the East; the walls are hung with engravings, copies of the great masters, including one of Raphael's Madonnas, Titian's Magdalena, Corregio's Magdalena, and so on. Over the mantelpiece a clock tells us what time it is getting to be. In the bookcase I find a respectable collection of classical and modern authors: Le Sage's 'Gil Blas,' Pope's works, Shakespeare's works, Tacitus, Dante in the original, Molière in the original, Lamartine's 'Histoire des Girondins,' Thiers' 'Consulat et l'Empire,' Walpole's letters, etc. Among the curios in the cabinet at which I looked inquisitively through the glass doors, I will mention some exquisitely beautiful pieces in mother-of-pearl, probably from Jerusalem, elegant baskets carved in wood, some mineral specimens, a piece of marble from the Parthenon, a stone model of an Egyptian mummy, an ostrich egg, water from the Jordan in a bottle, strange footwear. —Tea was served in extremely beautiful china cups but without teaspoons."

In connection with the commission that Hjalmar Hammarsköld had received to build the new State House in Columbia, he and his family had left Charleston and taken residence there, much missed by Rosalie, who on her visits to the city had always been invited to be their guest. This time she went to stay with the Logan family but was included everywhere in the invitations to visit the Peronneaus' relatives and friends. Writing in December from Charleston to the Hammarskölds in Columbia, she told of the regatta days on 23 and 24 November: "We were out in the harbor on a schooner positioned there for the use of the managers. Mr. Parker was one of them and on our arrival took charge of us and brought us up to the schooner, which had been readied to receive us and was supplied with refreshments in the form of cakes and oranges. It was a glorious day but almost too warm. The Battery, like the houses in the area, was draped with onlookers . . . the surface of the water was agitated by a multitude of small boats which crossed back and forth in all directions. The racing boats were all long, narrow, and very pointed, rowed by Negroes whose number varied between 8 and 12—that's true, the second day I saw a boat rowed by white men. The rowers wore a kind of uniform, some with red shirts and yellow neckerchiefs around the head, others blue and white jerseys, white neckerchiefs, and so on. There were five rounds of races, two the first day, three the second. There were no more than three boats at a time, and from the shore shouts of hurrah were sent up for the winner. The boats were under the command of gentlemen, and a little flag with their numbers had been placed in the stern of each of the boats. It was a pretty sight though not as exciting as we had supposed it would be, for we could not discern the distance growing between the boats until they were close to the goal. . . . First prize, if I am not mistaken, was $500, the smallest, $100."

On her return to "Dungannon," Rosalie shared with her mother, in a letter dated 16 November 1853, a privileged glimpse into Charlestonian society. "Repairs to the carriage and our friends' insistence led to our prolonging our stay in Charleston to two weeks. During that time I made the acquaintance of the Peronneau family's closest relatives and was admitted to Charleston's best society. They have just as aristocratic an attitude as European nobility, perhaps even more, for among the former, family counts for everything, while among the latter, money, talent, genius assume a hardly subordinate place. The [James] Ravenels are among the chief chickens in the basket and assume a thoroughly aristocratic attitude." However, Rosalie had to decline an invitation from them after a visit to a dentist, who "filled, and pulled several teeth," left her feeling spent. Dinner in the home of Mr. Thomas Coffin, Mrs. Peronneau's brother, was described as "quite stylish." "We were conveyed there at 3:30 in an elegant equipage, were conducted by the host, who is a widower, up to his drawing room, where we were received by his eldest daughter, an elegant young lady a little more than 20 years old. (She called her aunt's husband Mr. Peronneau!) At every cover there was a small bottle of water covered with a glass, three wine glasses and a quarter of a lemon. The guests squeezed several drops according to taste into the soup, which was served first, thick with meat as is usual in their soups; then fish with, what is unusual, Irish potatoes; then followed the meat courses, ... and then custard with sugar cake, quince preserves, and peaches as well as a kind of fruit tart. When that had been dispatched, the table was cleared, and the dessert, consisting of wine, oranges, apples, and pomegranates, was set out, after which a little crystal bowl containing an orange leaf to perfume the water was passed around to each one of the guests to wash his hands. The wines were Sherry, Madeira, and Sauterne. Later, we ascended to the drawing room, where we conversed, tried 'table moving,' and I played a little. I was utterly astonished to see coffee served after dinner; it is otherwise not the custom here.

"We went on from there to Mrs. Gibbs's, Mrs. Peronneau's sister, who is a widow with eight children, where we had been invited to tea. There was not as much elegance and etiquette there but more cordiality and liveliness. Tea was served with cakes, oranges, apples, and coconuts, and the time passed in conversation and games.

"One evening we were invited to a concert, quite good to be the Philharmonic Society of Charleston; they had in fact a full house but very few who understood or appreciated good music so that here and there someone was taking a nap, a good many yawned and wished that it was soon over. In fact, if I were an artist, I would not wish to give a concert in Charleston, for it is only the Negro singers who catch on with the public."

Rosalie had already become acquainted with "table moving" and related phenomena then having a vogue in America as she told of them in her letter from "Dungannon" of 1 May to "all my dear ones": "I must tell you now about 'spirit rappers,' who divert so many people in the United States and have now pitched their tent in Charleston and vicinity. You perhaps recall having read about them in our newspapers a few years ago. It involves a kind of curious communication with the spirit world which many believe in as though in the Bible, but I who have yet to see any proof am still among the nonbelievers. The form taken most popularly in these spiritual revelations is to let the tables walk, which proceeds in this manner: Several persons seat themselves around the table, preferably one with three feet, lay their hands flat on it so that they are all touching one another and thus form a continuous chain. Their clothing must not touch the table, and after they have sat in this fashion from 20 minutes to an hour, <u>it is claimed</u> that the table begins to move under their hands; when someone asks, 'Table, are you charged?' (that is, with electricity) the table replies by means of raising one corner, which when repeated three times means 'yes.' The question then follows, 'Is so and so the medium?' and the table replies affirmatively in the manner just described, negatively by remaining immobile. Then can be asked whatever one pleases, and the answers are supplied in the same fashion; the person who is the medium can make the table move along in any direction whatever by holding a finger on it—indeed, stories are told of tables that stroll in this manner up and down the stairs. Dr. Logan, who knows a woman who is a medium, maintains that the table which she charged lifted at his request the leg which was nearest him and gave him a blow on the shoulder. I scarcely believe that there is any group of people in Charleston who have not tried to get tables to move. We also have experimented but without success; we followed all the established rules and sat for a whole hour without noticing the least movement of the table. It is impossible for me to believe in any of it until I see it myself, but I have heard many insist on the mobility of tables as a truth explained by electricity, which is conveyed to them by the human body.

"Dr. de Saussure, a relative of the Peronneaus, was going to give us convincing proof the other day, and a table did indeed move, but it was through a strong though almost imperceptible movement of his wrist, which I nevertheless noticed. Although at first he denied it, he finally had to admit that that was how it had happened, adding that that was the entire secret. But others objected to this in the most serious way and told of amazing proofs of the prophetical powers of tables. But, anyway, I must see before I can believe. These mediums are called 'moving mediums,' and another sort are 'rapping mediums,' who by means of rappings have their questions answered, and a third kind are 'writing mediums,' who themselves write the answers which are supplied to them, like the oracles, by an invisible power. Dr. Logan's father is wholly convinced and often goes to a medium in order to talk through her with his deceased wife. His son has seen several of the answers that have been furnished, some of them composed in verse."

Christmas customs in Charleston were a subject in which Rosalie took a special interest in two letters to her mother. In one, which was dated 23 January 1854, she recalled after the fact some of the curious behavior she had witnessed. "Winter here is the time for the city dwellers to go visiting in the country, because they scarcely dare venture in the summer beyond the city limits unless they travel to 'the North.' Many families go north every year. Christmas is especially the time when all city dwellers endeavor to get out into the country, and they are not the least discommoded at being away from home, for they often are members of a family scattered about in different places. Christmas is the Negroes' great treat, for their winter clothing is handed out to them then, and they usually have some extra entertainment provided, and also have three days free. On Christmas Eve they were here to get their clothes, and it was a beautiful and animated sight. Each one of the women also got a gift of a beautiful neckerchief. Mr. E[dward] Parker placed silver coins on a rock and had the men run and pick them up. The women also ran in a race for a quarter dollar. It was enjoyable to see how this took place quietly without quarreling, interrupted only by their shouts of laughter. There is really less commotion and crudeness among the Negroes than among the lower classes at home." Rosalie's other letter to her mother about Christmas customs was written as the season was still approaching its climax, 18 December 1853: "Our circle of new members consisting of relatives and friends increased the whole time before Christmas, but I have scarcely time to enjoy their company, for I have not yet grown out of my old habit of taking on a great deal and thinking that I have time for more than I can manage. We were going to celebrate Christmas in Swedish style with Christmas gifts and a Christmas tree. I had made this suggestion partly to provide some fun for the girls, partly to get them to engage in some fine handwork, for nothing of that sort gets done when they are at their studies, partly because they have so much to study, partly because they are not careful to make good use of their time. It was precisely for this last reason that much of their work was postponed until the last moment, which resulted in haste on their part and dissatisfaction on that of their visitors, who did not like to see them so diligent, for industry is in general not one of the chief virtues of American ladies. This dissatisfaction, along with the quantity of work which I had both on my own account and to get into order for the girls, gave rise to some unpleasantness for me and also taught me a couple of good lessons: the one is not to try to introduce new customs, the other not to attempt oneself more than one can bring to completion. I got it all finished, however, but had to work hard."

Everyone in the family and all the guests were to have a small gift; among the many things that were produced were undersleeves of tulle, ribbons and lace, embroidered collars, pin cushions and books of needles, a purse made of silk moiré and silver, memorandum books, and a chessboard painted with every other square in blue with landscapes in white and India ink, and every other one white with flowers, all squares different. Christmas Eve fell on a Saturday, and rather than risk not getting permission to let the Sabbath interrupt the festivities, it was decided, to Rosalie's great relief, to postpone the Christmas celebration until Monday. Her hurry was still so great on Monday that she did not want to go down and join the others at Christmas dinner, so that the master of the house himself kindly carried up food to her in her room. He also had sent to Charleston for two boxes which had just arrived from Sweden containing

Christmas gifts for the entire Peronneau family, and for Rosalie a portrait in oils of her father, and including also "a jar of lingonberry preserves and sausage that Mutter dear had made herself." This time the captain had fortunately made a speedy voyage and everything arrived in excellent condition. "It was not until 10 o'clock that the Christmas tree and gifts were ready and the 'toss-in'[1] began. This was an amusement completely new to them and aroused much merriment especially when the greeting written on the package included something clever.

"There then starts up a noble effort to reciprocate the Roos family's good will and within a few minutes we had a box packed to the brim with gifts. . . . In addition, I am sending you a lot of flower seeds as well as birds' eggs for Thure and a little rattlesnake in Spiritus Vino for Leonard. And also a box of sweet potatoes packed in sand which we had great trouble getting dry, and two jars of preserves, one of peaches and the other of tomatoes. Oh, may it all get to you undamaged!"

Writing to her sister 18 February 1854, Rosalie had still more to relate of festivities during the holidays. "There was a big party at one of our neighbors. I was soberly attired in a black silk dress open in front and with short sleeves, and a chemisette and short undersleeves with pink ribbons and lace, swan's-down ruffles, and a headdress of black velvet and pink ribbon. We did not get there until between 7 and 8 and waited a good while until the other guests arrived; isn't that delay really absurd? The interior was comfortably furnished with beautiful rugs, easy chairs, and comfortable seats. The daughter of our host was dressed in a pale mauve, fresh-looking silk dress, but most of them wore white with flowers in their hair. After a time the guests assembled, and the dance began. The music consisted of a violin, hardly superior to our celebrated fiddler in Klefva, a tambourine, and a triangle, which instruments together produced rather ear-piercing sounds. The company was not large, but could boast of several beautiful well-dressed girls. . . . There was, on the other hand, no one outstanding among the gentlemen, except perhaps Mr. Edward Parker and Mr. William Henry Peronneau, and I missed in most of them a certain elegance and tournure which I like to see and prefer to good looks. In comparison with the ladies the gentlemen did not look dressed in their

---

[1] Literal translation of *inkastandet*, described by Rosalie in the Limestone school paper as a Christmas Eve custom at "Sjögerås." The larger gifts were placed under a Christmas tree; smaller gifts, each bearing the name of its recipient and a little Christmas doggerel, were distributed by someone dressed as the *jultomte*, the Christmas elf, who knocked loudly and then tossed the gifts into the house, whereupon everyone rushed outdoors to try to intercept him.

frock coats and dark vests. The dance began with a quadrille, a boulanger, and a reel without a change of partners; a waltz was struck up but only two couples danced, for the waltz, poletta, and schottische are danced by very few and seldom at balls. Between times, the girls like to dance them, and if they permit a partner to lead, it is only by holding them by the hands, crosswise. They would look with complete disgust at the way we dance, and if an American woman of the proper sort should attend one of our balls, she surely would faint in horror. After a while, however, they tired of the sameness of their dances, and our host's daughter came and asked me to teach them some Swedish dances. I showed them the clap anglaise and afterwards was going to try the regular anglaise, but they thought that too difficult to master. I had a rather good time, danced most of the dances, but I always feel so much alone in such large gatherings, for as at home the girls flocked together. You probably think it strange that I use the word 'girls' in this fashion as though to suggest that I do not count myself among them. So in fact it is, for for me to be called a girl would be regarded as highly 'disrespectful.' As soon as they have turned 20 and even before, they have grown out of that denomination and are 'young ladies.'

"There were no refreshments passed around, but wine and cakes had been placed on a table to which the cavaliers escorted their ladies if they so desired. The gentlemen conversed with the ladies between dances, and if someone was asked to play, she was led to the piano by her partner. Supper was ready at 1 o'clock, when each one escorted his lady and helped her to what she wished. Dr. Logan was my 'beau,' as they are called. . . . Supper was served in a frigid little room, and of course, poor me, I minded the cold greatly. We stood clustered around the table which was completely covered with turkey, ducks, ham, chicken, chicken salad, oyster pâté, bread and butter, cloudberry jelly, blancmange, ice cream, cakes, and on small silver dishes scattered everywhere on the table, various confections commonly called sugarplums; in addition, champagne and other wines. One selects in no special order whatever strikes the fancy, and consequently it happens that many begin with ice cream and end with ham. It is not until the ladies have finished and the gentlemen have escorted them back to the drawing room and parlor that the latter begin their supper. A little after supper we set out on our return journey and arrived home at 4.

"From having attended these parties the girls had acquired a taste for them, and as in old times at home, they began to bear down on their elders to obtain their consent to give a party here. After several demurs, they succeeded. Mrs. Peronneau herself was by no means in favor of the idea but had to give in, and the young ones drew up long lists of things which their father had to secure, and they assumed full command over the household stores. You must realize, you see, that in America it is not the parents who control the children but the children who control the parents. More than once I have heard with astonishment and displeasure how the former contradict and at times criticize the latter. But as Papa says, 'Vive la république.'

"In the meantime great preparations were being made, a quantity of things were brought from the city . . . invitations were sent out also to several young gentlemen in the city.

"Mrs. William Henry Peronneau and her sister-in-law assumed command of the household and held sway over the pantry, where our Mrs. Peronneau looked in not one time. Do you suppose our mother would have given in so easily? . . . The first Thursday of the new year was the big day. The day before, we had made garlands of cypress and holly and hung them over the windows in the drawing room and parlor as well as over the wide doorways between these rooms. . . .

"Our white dresses were freshly ironed and carried up to our rooms, but we were all of us still down in the storeroom, everyone in full motion. I had iced the fruit cake which looked quite impressive; we had spread several dozen sandwiches; a cart had arrived from the Parkers and had been unloaded; glasses and porcelain were being carefully washed when the Parkers showed up. What news do you suppose they brought with them? Nothing less than that Mr. P's aunt, on either his mother's or his father's side, had died the night before and so no party could take place! It is true that she was almost unknown to the family, but the relationship was too close, and since her family lived in Charleston, it could not have been kept secret from them that there had been a dance here the day after she died.

"The consternation of the young people could not have been greater if lightning had struck, and Eliza was almost in tears. Cancellations were now sent out in all directions, . . . but the evening was nevertheless spent rather merrily, for we had no fewer than 17 young people in the house. There was dancing and games here every evening as long as they stayed. . . . The last guests did not leave until 31 January, when Eliza also went along to attend the balls which are given in Charleston during February; that month is their carnival time and actually the only one when they pleasure themselves. Eliza's eldest brother escorted her to these balls, for the mothers seldom go 'out in company,' as it is called, with their daughters here, but most often the brothers, even the unmarried ones, perform the service of chaperons. At some public balls it is said that older women are never present.

"Actually, I am just as well pleased to be back in peace and quiet; I am better off when I am working than going to parties. . . . It has also been difficult to get the girls back to work again and still worse to get them up in the mornings."

To a question from home whether she had read Fredrika Bremer's newly published *Homes in the New World*, Rosalie had replied 16 November 1853: "No, but I have heard a great deal said about it and not favorably. Through it, the author has lost the popularity which she had won with her fiction, and they criticize her severely for having broken the laws of hospitality, failed in tact, indulged in jest incompatible with good taste, gone about everywhere prying so that even the servants 'got disgusted with her.' I heard one woman go so far as to call her 'abominable.' It pained me to hear it, and I am sorry if an author whom we all revere is really guilty of the charges that have been brought against her. They say that she has mixed too many persons up in her work, named people's names, ridiculed people in whose houses she had enjoyed kindness, placed private conversations in the public domain, and in a word, she is criticized and derided as much as she had previously been praised and loved. There is scarcely any middle course existing here, for here more than elsewhere it can be said that 'les extrêmes se touchent'; it is simply 'I love or I hate.' In general the Americans here in the South are very good, friendly, polite, and helpful to strangers, but they think highly of themselves and if you wound their self-esteem, the friendly feelings are soon exchanged for anger and scorn. I will soon read her book and judge for myself."

IX

AMERICA AS DREAM AND REALITY

Once again it was Rosalie's father who required information going beyond the domestic arrangements in America that she so often mentioned in her correspondence. In a letter to him from "Dungannon," 12 January 1854, Rosalie wrote: "It is strange to see how these words are confirmed everywhere: 'One only wants to have what one does not have, and what one has does not enjoy.' Thus, for example, you regard the form of government in the United States as being the best and wish to be informed of its merits, whereas Mr. Peronneau and others dislike it and assure me that it will not last out another century. He says that the only possibility for the republic to continue is the existence of slavery, for otherwise the power will fall into the hands of the brutish, uneducated masses. He calls me a republican. The general elections, which seem so desirable to those at home, give rise here to many intrigues and shameful acts, for it is not the worthiest who is elected but the one who can buy the most votes. Mr. Hammarsköld says therefore that if he was a liberal before, he now would be the most conservative man if he should ever return to Sweden." Later in the letter, she commented on her father's wish that she secure a job in Charleston for his youngest son. "I frankly admit that I would not at all care to see one of my brothers as a clerk in a store, and that would be the only job Wickenberg[1] could give him. Perhaps you shake your head and say 'pride,' but it is not that sin which causes me to be opposed to such a course, but its depressing effect on someone with a higher education. I would therefore much prefer to see my brothers in such positions where they could improve their intellectual capabilities and increase their store of knowledge as well as refine their taste, and you must admit that there is no opportunity for that for someone who has no other occupation from early in the morning until late in the evening than to weigh spices and victuals. I certainly do not mean by this that he who is so occupied is less worthy than a man of science, for it is the man who ennobles the labor, not the labor the man. . . . To be sure, money is important; it is perhaps one of the essentials for a happy life, but it cannot secure happiness, and I confess

---

1 Carl Johan Wickenberg, a Swedish merchant in Charleston (Mrs. Laurell's note).

that I would feel better hearing that my brothers are counted among the most intelligent men rather than among the richest. I bow most deeply not before aristocrats of birth nor of wealth, but before aristocrats of the world of the mind. . . . I trust that after what I have now expressed you will no longer attribute my objections to pride rising out of class differences, but only to a desire that my brothers may advance beyond the average with respect to intellect." As for her father's suggestion that she try to secure a place for his son in an office, Rosalie replied: "Good places are hard to find, and even if one were obtained, no salary can be counted on in the first years. Mr. Peronneau estimates the cost in such a case to be about $500 a year if he should live modestly. He says also that Swedes have a good reputation here and are preferred to Germans and often to natives. Much importance is attached to the knowledge of foreign languages since in general the natives are not much at home in them. What requires improvement is Gustaf's handwriting, and I would seriously recommend a course in penmanship as being highly urgent."

To the brother who was the subject of all these plans Rosalie herself wrote, 21 January 1854: "You know of old with what partiality Papa has always regarded America and how eagerly he has wished that one of his sons would get the benefit of the advantages it has in his eyes over the old world. Whether all these advantages are as great as he imagines them to be, I shall not go into here, for I do not believe myself capable of passing judgment on them. Certainly, however, those objects at which we look through the telescope of the imagination take on a rosy glow, a kind of aura which disappears when we approach more closely to the reality; but much of value can nevertheless remain even after the aura has faded. So it is with America; we of the old world find here much which does not answer our expectations, does not coincide with our views, and offends our prejudices, but also much that is good and useful, perhaps better than what we left behind. I do not doubt that a steady young man, hardworking and persevering and of high principles, can be successful, as it is called, more quickly here than at home; the resources are vaster, the rewards are larger, but if he does not possess the above-mentioned qualities, he will be all the sooner headed toward his downfall, will fall farther than he would elsewhere. America is a land of contrasts: refinement and crudeness, luxury and misery, high virtue and profound immorality exist side by side more closely here than in Europe."

These sober reflections were momentarily forgotten in the exhilaration of personal achievement that swept into a letter to another brother, Axel, in the early days of March 1854, when Rosalie confided things she had never before dared to imagine, much less speak of. "It is odd indeed that so much of what I eagerly wished for in my childhood and early youth but which I had not the least reason to suppose could be fulfilled has now become reality. First of all, I had a passion for travel, especially beyond the European area, and I supposed in those days, when my imagination colored every object with the brightest of colors, that a journey to the new world across the great ocean would be the height of bliss. The South and a more tropical climate with its warm sun and rich vegetation seemed especially alluring, and with what interest did I not read every description of the region and its inhabitants that fell into my hands! And now here I sit in South Carolina, enjoying its early spring, its luxuriant vegetation, and feeling myself at ease with the daily life of its people—and what is more, I hope to be able to see much more of this hemisphere's many wonders, for having once flown the coop, nothing seems impossible.

"After having read Mrs. Pfeiffer's 'Voyage Round the World,'[2] I even had some fleeting thoughts of traveling to Brazil and from there to the west coast of South America and on to China and South Asia. I reasoned thus: what one person has been able to do is not impossible for another, and do I not have the same energy, the same capabilities, the same strength as that German lady? Besides, I have one advantage over her, namely a score of years fewer to be afflicted by, at the same time that I feel myself to be old enough, experienced, and independent enough to venture out on my own. So do not be altogether too surprised in case you should hear that your dear sister has set out on a voyage to Japan, Borneo, or such unchristian places. However, do not let my <u>wild</u> suggestions get out of the family!

"But back to former desires and their truly wonderful fulfillment. <u>Independence</u> was also one of my dreams that I supposed would be impossible to realize, and more than once I felt a kind of envy of the happy, free, independent situation that men enjoy and thought with a sigh that I would have to be dependent all my life. Yet now, I am more independent than any of my brothers, for in the first place I earn my own livelihood, and in the second I feel no other restraints on my free will to do and to help out just as I please than those which reason and a sense of justice impose upon me. . . .

"I have always had a thirst for knowledge, and the desire to increase what I have already acquired and to add to it has constantly been alive in my mind. The study of languages has especially delighted me, and many

2 Ida Pfeiffer was the author of many books of travel including *A Lady's Voyage Round the World*, translated from the German (London, 1851; New York, 1852); entitled in other editions *A Woman's Journey Round the World* (London, 1850, etc.).

times I deemed those persons fortunate who could express themselves with facility in a foreign language. With respect to knowledge, I have gained considerably during the period of 2½ years I have spent in America. . . . I have learned something else of importance, namely to make good use of my time; necessity is a good teacher.

"In the past I often asserted that an unmarried woman could accomplish more good than a married one; I plan now to prove that in deeds. Like you, I need constantly to be doing something in order to be happy, and of the two alternatives I would rather attempt a little too much than too little. Nor is this activity to be limited to the material world; it must also involve the mind.

"I once had indefinite dreams of becoming an author, for the good that I could contribute thereby, the honor and the fame that I would acquire. My dreams begin now to assume a more definite form, and although the desire for fame would no longer be a motivation for my entering the lists of life, I do not regard it as impossible that I shall sometime take that step. . . . I also have another long-cherished plan for the future, but its fulfillment probably will encounter several obstacles." Evidently Rosalie was referring here to an institute in Sweden for the higher education of women, which she mentioned in a letter to her former teacher, Maria Magdalena Schenson. Her letter to Axel continued:

"Sometimes the interval between these two periods seems like a dream, a happy, bright, playful dream, followed by painful disillusionment. Sometimes I wonder if I ought not to see in this the finger of Providence and follow the path it seems to point out to me. As a married woman I would have become too conscientious in the fulfillment of my responsibilities to have the least thought of literary activities; unmarried, I have no one to think ill of me if I should devote my life and my powers to them and in that way pay my mite to society. How strangely has not the one event in my life been linked to the other! In my travels and in the incidents connected to them I see more clearly the guidance of Providence than in anything else, . . . how does it not seem that the one obstacle after the other fell away of itself!

"During the year just past and the one I spent at Limestone, I never busied myself with poetry; I neither had time nor felt the desire. This year the old desire has awakened, and during my solitary rambles I improvise small verses which I put down on paper on my return home—indoors I never have time to work on my poetry.

"But I am afraid that I am boring you with all my chatter about myself! You see, I have no one to whom I can talk confidentially and without reservation; when therefore I let the pent-up stream flow unchecked, it pours forth joyously and tumultuously and perhaps is continued longer than it should be. . . .

"The news from here is now rather sparse, for after the noisy Christmas holidays we have returned to our former quiet routine. Sometimes it is interrupted by one or another gentleman friend of Mr. Peronneau's out traveling, who stays over for the night, or Dr. Logan comes on a visit. Clelia takes particular satisfaction in such interruptions, for she can then at least see 'a new face, as she is perfectly tired up [*sic*] of the old ones.' "

Rosalie had ominous news for her mother when she wrote to her on 20 March 1854: "I was planning to spend the last half of April in Columbia, but we shall see how that turns out, for poor Emilie has been and still is very ill. During the time the legislature was meeting in Columbia in the autumn, the Hammarskölds provided several of its members with board and lodging. Emilie, who has now taken charge of the household, saw to everything herself, worked like a dog—as she herself expressed it—and for a period of three weeks prepared a feast every day for 18 persons at table, stood in the mornings at the kitchen range and then played l'aimable in the evenings in the parlor, but her strength finally failed her, her old headaches returned worse than ever, and since 18 December she has been extremely ill and almost blind." One week later, Emilie Hammarsköld's life came to an end, and Rosalie made a journey of quite another sort to Columbia than had been planned. She met there with the grief-stricken family and Hedda Hammarsköld from Spring Hill. They all joined in an earnest appeal to Rosalie to come and assume the care of the motherless children. Writing from Columbia 7 April 1854 to her mother, Rosalie told of her dilemma: "It is awfully, awfully hard to reply negatively to their pleas, tears, and more than eloquent glances, but on the other side there is the Peronneau family and the obligations which I have to them. It is truly a difficult situation; it seems to me just as hard to say yes as to say no—oh, if only someone would decide for me. . . . I feel also that I owe a debt of gratitude to Hjalmar, who with such true kindness came to meet me when I arrived here a total stranger. . . . Tant Hedda herself will write to Mrs. Peronneau and give an account of all these circumstances for her earnest consideration . . . and I mean to talk with her as soon as I get home, leave Tant's letter with her, and beg her to tell me what she thinks I should do." Rosalie, now at "Bentwood," in the Pineland, continued in a letter of 20 May to her mother: "It came as a wholly unexpected blow to the Peronneaus, and although they said that they did not wish to oppose my moving if I wished, they nevertheless said that, given general opinion and prevailing prejudices here, such a step would be unsuitable in the highest degree and that I would expose myself to general censure and lay myself open to unpleasant rumors by going to live with a widower to take care of his children. The presence of his mother-in-law in the home was not enough to protect my reputation. If you know me, Mother, you will understand how much I suffered from these circumstances. On the one hand, my poor friends who have so many claims on my friendship and gratitude, . . . on the other hand, the Peronneaus and the debt of gratitude which I owe them, and the girls' unfinished education, which with my move would suffer a sudden interruption. Thought of the world's judgment and of my being the object of slander never entered my head . . . and it was as though my uncertainty had placed my character in an ambiguous light. . . . Mr. Peronneau, who certainly had no selfish desire to detain me, had asked the advice of several of his friends, and 'it will by no means do' was the uniform answer."

In connection with these events Rosalie wrote a candid letter to Hedda Hammarsköld 1 June 1854: "If only Mrs. Peronneau had said to me, 'The world will condemn your actions, but we shall approve them. Carry on elsewhere, doing more than can be done here; be strong and take courage against vicious slander. We shall speak well of you; we shall respect and love you wherever you may go.' With that assurance I would have met the world's slander with head held high, for when my friends believed in me, what would the blame of strangers matter? Realizing this gave me courage to defy the world's opinion when I left home for America; prejudice is also powerful and strong there, and there too slander and calumny aim their blows at the innocent as well as the guilty. . . . And in evidence of this I need only refer to Professor Olivecrona's remark to Hulda: 'Recently one of Malla's acquaintances, Mlle. Roos, has also gone off to America; since she did not succeed in getting a man at home, she wants to see whether she will have better luck there.' These thoughtless words wounded me very deeply, for at that time I was much more sensitive than now, my heart still sick and easily moved; it was so much the worse since I had always felt confounded by women ambitious to get married. . . . Although insinuations having to do with marriage are still always unpleasant and hurtful since I am indeed much too proud and have in mind for myself too serene a life ever to stoop to the level of such speculations, I can nevertheless snap my fingers at the utterances of Prof. Olivecrona and his ilk, for I know that none of my friends entertain any such suspicions." Rosalie reacted strongly also to Mrs. Peronneau's remark to Hedda Hammarsköld that she supposed that Rosalie ought to find sufficient fulfillment of her mission in life in being the governess to the Peronneau daughters. "That really upset me, and I must admit that my aspirations are higher, for my sphere of activity here has been too restricted to be able to satisfy my yearnings in this matter. For what is in fact my calling here? Clearly not to prepare young hearts for a higher life in heaven or for lofty accomplishments on earth, but to stimulate their talents and impart knowledge to them, no doubt agreeable to have but in no way necessary for their true happiness. I have too little authority over them to give direction to or to mold their character, nor is this easily done with an American girl accustomed from infancy to be self-indulgent and independent. They sometimes regard even their lenient and submissive mother as too strict; how would they then look upon my meddling in the most important part of their rearing. . . . Torn between conflicting claims, after tears and bitter hours, . . . I wrote finally a negative answer to my dear, beloved friends."

Rosalie continued in her letter of 20 May to her mother: "I am happy that mail for foreign delivery is managed better than domestic mail, which is unforgivably mishandled. Two letters from Spring Hill went astray before my trip to Columbia. Since coming back, I have written three times to them, but the other day I had a letter from Tant expressing her sadness and concern in not having heard the least thing from me since our separation. Too annoying for words! . . . We have moved out to the Pineland again; it is quiet and still here but rich in pines and flowers. The girls, however, fuss indescribably; they do not appreciate their good fortune in having a good home. . . . The worst drawbacks here, as it seems to me, are the dust and the water. The former is as fine as ash and black as soot; the latter has the strong taste of marsh water, and the other day a huge black snake slipped down into the well; I shudder now every time I take a drink, can't get the snake out of my mind."

Rosalie wrote two far-ranging letters to her father that summer, the first on 25 May: "Those are appalling stories about the mail robbery and the prison riots which you tell me, and it is melancholy to hear of the existence of such things in my beloved fatherland, but sad to say, misery and crime exist everywhere in the new as well as the old world. The story of the Negroes who were hunted to death by bloodhounds in the neighborhood of Charleston, of which I gave you an account in a previous letter [not preserved], occupies so high a position in the annals of crime that for atrociousness it can be surpassed only with difficulty. And, Papa dear, the misery and extravagance in Stockholm fade to nothing in comparison to New York, where the former is said to be limitless, and the latter without restraint. Think of a dress costing $1000!. . .

"We get newspapers here three times a week. Mr. Peronneau subscribes to one published in Charleston called 'The Mercury.' It, like the other Charleston papers, mostly contains advertisements; the ones I am familiar with are 'Evening News' and 'The Courier.' One of the New York newspapers which is widely read and well edited is the 'New York Herald'; many people also get the London 'Times' and the English 'Punch.' The best periodical being published in the United States is 'Harper's Magazine.'. . . . I have so little time for reading that I cannot keep up, but Mr. Peronneau always tells me when there is important news from Europe." Rosalie nevertheless found time for a second, even longer letter to her father, 26 June, in which she gave further thought to travel plans. "The main theme of your letter was travel, and since I am also giving much thought to that subject and draw up more or less impracticable plans, I shall make room here for that subject. I cannot say that I am fearful of traveling alone, for I believe that God's hand guides me just as lovingly then, but I feel a kind of uneasiness doing so and consider the first step especially to be the most difficult. . . . The greatest difficulty, however, rests in my naturally timid temperament, the dread I feel of pushing my way forward and of coming into contact with rude, uncultivated beings. I have really not yet been out on my own, for I have always had some helpful person to look after me and thus have avoided until now travel likely to invite trouble. But I know it cannot always be so if I wish to see more of America; . . . it is always most difficult to become emancipated from the influence of prejudices in a place of which you have been an inextricable part and where you may have many friends. You always feel easier and freer to act where you are a stranger. And do not believe for one moment that the Americans are a people without prejudices, for that is a complete mistake. The prejudices here are even more stubborn, and the most inveterate aristocrats at home do not talk more about family, good and old, about 'société comme il faut,' than republican Americans. The Peronneau family has uncompromisingly aristocratic tendencies, and since I am regarded by them as a lady of 'good family,' they are horrified by my thinking that I can travel on my own. Once I have broken the ice and have ventured forth, I do not think it will be so hard. I am healthy and strong, completely at home in the language, and believe that through acquaintances I can obtain letters of introduction for use in several of the large cities. As far as helping myself with respect to clothes is concerned, I shall feel no embarrassment because I have long been accustomed to it. I shall send direct from Charleston one of my large trunks with books and things that I do not wish to get rid of, . . . and then I intend to travel with two small light trunks and perhaps a hat box (don't ever imagine that a woman can travel without such an article!). I would be very happy if you could obtain information for me about the cost of traveling between New Orleans and New York by way of the western states and also if you could obtain from Mlle. Bremer a couple of letters of introduction to some of her acquaintances along the way since I do not know anyone who has relatives there. . . .

"You ask how the church is organized in this country. It is so organized that it does not exist. I have not been to church this year other than in Charleston and Columbia. There are a couple of churches 10 miles from here in a summer place inhabited by planters who have had to leave their plantations in the warm season. Partly because of the heat and the distance to travel there, partly because the horses are often afflicted with ailments. In St. Andrew's Parish, where Mr. Parker's family lives, there is a church and a priest, but since his health is frail, services there cannot be depended upon every Sunday. If I am not mistaken, his entire salary consists of pew rents. The state, which has nothing to do with the church, builds no temples, ordains no priests, but all this is done through the congregations, which try to win adherents to their sect, or by private individuals. There are also priests of various sects who travel about preaching, sometimes rather poor stuff. One such, as bony, thin, and cadaverous as [Rev. Carl] Theorell, preaches to Mr. Peronneau's Negroes every third Sunday for a salary of $20 or $25 for the year. He preaches every Sunday at four different places, and the income he receives is scarcely enough to sustain his family." During her most recent visit to Charleston, Rosalie had been present at the dedication of a Unitarian Church: "The sermon included an account of the rise of the Unitarian Church and of the reaction to it by other sects. The preacher almost tore to pieces several tenets of faith of Trinitarian churches and gave me a very clear representation of what the Unitarians <u>did not believe</u>. <u>What</u> they do believe never became clear to me, however. In the first place, he disputed the doctrine of the Trinity as something absurd and without support in the Bible. . . . The Unitarians seem to conceive of our doctrine of the Trinity in a completely materialistic way, not as various manifestations by which God reveals himself. . . . They also deny original sin, redemption through Our Savior, and faith as a condition for our salvation. On the latter point they are in direct opposition to the Baptists, who say that faith does everything, and that for a reformed person to be saved he may do whatever he pleases if only he believes in the divinity of Christ. This faith can be indeed dangerous to ignorant people without principles. Moreover, the Baptists are not highly regarded by other believers; the Unitarians, however, are in general morally good people, for they believe that their fate in the world to come depends entirely on their good deeds. . . . <u>What</u> they believe about Christ and how they believe in Him remain a secret to me, however. They receive communion in His memory but deny His divinity. . . . Several persons with whom I have spoken about this also say that the Unitarians do not have any real creed and scarcely know themselves what they believe in. Many Trinitarians regard them almost as heathens; in fact I have heard several persons say they would rather be Catholics or Jews than Unitarians.

"But to return to the sermon—I thought it would never come to an end, and half the congregation was napping, while the priests glanced a bit anxiously at one another."

Rosalie had already had much to say on the question of religious differences in America in a letter addressed to "all my dear ones," 24 May 1854. "There is a very strong prejudice against the Catholics. . . . The cause of this hatred of the Papists, as the Catholics are often called, is no doubt to be attributed to the persecution they instituted against Protestant adherents who finally left house and home and fatherland in order to worship the Supreme Being in accordance with their convictions. America offered such a haven, and in its forests the Huguenots and the Puritans raised their temples without being troubled by fanaticism and bigotry, but they left as a legacy to their descendants their hatred of the oppressors, and they in turn have great difficulty suppressing their animosity toward a 'Roman Catholic.' . . . The Baptist church is said to have the largest membership, then come the Methodists, the Presbyterians, finally the Episcopalians. These are the foremost and numerically the strongest. Less numerous are the Catholics, Lutherans, Unitarians, Universalists, and Quakers. Included in the last is a sect called the Shaking Quakers, who dance and shake. I heard a woman describe them who had visited a colony near Lebanon in New York State. They are communists and thus hold everything in common; they live together in large buildings; their dress, their food, their household goods are all very simple but remarkably neat. The furniture in their bedrooms consists of one bed, one chair, one table. Everything they require they make themselves. They do not have marriages. Their church is a large room, completely empty, only some benches for visitors. And when they have assembled, they begin to dance. Then those preach who have been moved by the spirit.

"In consequence of this confusion of various sects and the controversies among them, there are many who never belong to any congregation and live and die without making confession to any church. I thank God for having been born in a country where a state religion prevails and where the youth are reared in accordance with it, for there are many here without religion only because they do not know which is the best, and sometimes also because they shy away from the duties and obligations which many churches demand of their members. Out in the country the churches are so far apart that many people never go to church. If the parents, therefore, are not pious, their children grow up in complete ignorance of religious subjects, and probably there is more than one American who could go along with the answer of an old woman to whom Mr. Curtis gave a Bible, asking her if she had heard anything about Jesus Christ: 'Please tell me who that is; I live so far away from the world that I do not know what is happening.'

"In general I do not care for the priests here—they are too dry and dogmatic, have too little feeling; but at St. Philip's there is a young priest to whom I listen with pleasure. One evening we went to a Presbyterian church. The preacher was rather well-spoken but somewhat too much given to declamation, and his sermon preached not in the spirit that I prefer, that I think of as Christian. His text was the story of John the Baptist and it gave him the opportunity to denounce birthday parties, dancing, etc."

Rosalie had more to say about religion and churches to her brother Axel in a letter of 13 August 1854: "No commandment is broken so much at home than the one which has to do with the observance of the Sabbath, and none is observed more strictly here. Many go so far as to think it a sin to take a walk in God's glorious creation, that they will not pick a flower or fruit on Sundays, that they will not even prepare food; and to read anything other than a Sunday book is thought to be extremely wrong. But they see nothing objectionable to sleeping a good part of the day which is dedicated to the glory of God, not even to taking a nap in church, nor to speaking foolishly and vaingloriously, nor to complaining that the day is long and boring. The keeping of the Sabbath correctly and appropriately is a subject to which we at home devote very little attention. . . . Christ modified the strict injunctions of the Mosaic law, but never did He nullify it. . . . Accustomed from childhood to see this day used for all sorts of diversions and amusements, I never once gave it a thought that that was anything wrong, although at times, when Sunday was taken up more than usual with worldly concerns, I could not suppress my wonder that this way of spending the Sabbath could be reconciled with the commandment: Keep the Sabbath holy. I thought further that if I were ever to have my own home to manage, there would be no big parties to prevent the family or the servants from attending church services. Even in this respect I would wish to hit upon a middle course. . . .

"For me the main tenet of religion is an inexpressible, all-embracing forgiving love which I most clearly and purely read in the great book of nature written with the Creator's own hand, the text at times in the stars, at times in the flowers, but everywhere always beautiful, always speaking to my heart; I read it also in the kindness all about me, in the lives that I encounter and which, when they are difficult to bear or delightful to receive, nevertheless redound finally to the best in me; I read it also, though not so clearly, in the creations of human genius, for does not every good gift come from the Father of light and is not genius a good and precious gift? Indeed, I say with the author of *Corinne*, 'Laissons nous donc tout confrondre, amour, réligion, génie et le soleil, et les parfumes, et la musique et la poésie; il n'y a d'athéisme que dans la froideur, l'égoisme, la bassesse.'[3] From this point of view I do not see God with my inward eye as a strict, demanding, implacable sovereign whose commands I obey in fear, but as an all-good father, whose arms are always ready to receive me, to whom I can continually flee with childlike trust and whose remembrance is as dear and sacred to me in the day of happiness as in the day of sorrow. Religion is therefore for me not a dead letter, not a formula devised by men which I listen to and repeat because that is as it shall be, but a living spirit which lives and works in me and whose presence I feel even in the course of my everyday occupations. It is the heart's warm, freely given, uninterrupted worship of the Creator which I would call the fear of God and not these cold, dead forms which prescribe certain words, certain trivial rules, but leave my heart unmoved, for the letter killeth, but the spirit giveth life."

To her "beloved friends" Rosalie had given, 27 July 1854, a glimpse into the social conventions of the society to which the Peronneaus had introduced her. "The Peronneau family, about whose origins Papa asks, is descended from French Huguenot nobility who left their fatherland upon the revocation of the Edict of Nantes. Many Frenchmen left their homes then and several of them settled here, having been welcomed by the settlers already present. There are many families here with French names like Ravenel, Lanneau, Legaré, de Saussure, etc., and these enjoy a very aristocratic status. In general, prejudices as to class and birth are much stronger than at home. It is not enough to know what kind of person someone is, but it's a question of who his ancestors were whether he can be received in the best society or not.

"'The best society of Charleston' consists of families descended from good English stock, in part those who distinguished themselves in the Revolution, in part Puritans and French Huguenots, and through family connections this society sticks together like a matted tangle of yarn. I do not know of any of these families who cannot trace relationships with the

---

3 "Let us, then, blend everything together: love, religion, genius, and the sun, and perfumes, and music and poetry; there is atheism only in frigidity, egoism, pettiness."

others if only they take the trouble. In Charleston wealth does not smooth the way to 'the best society' as it does in Europe or in the northern states. Nor is that the case with those who hold the highest positions in the state. . . . Mr. Peronneau takes the greatest pains in selecting the company his daughters keep: his criteria are, first, spotless morals; second, education; third, refined manners. He does not, however, think that all this can be found in every individual but in the individual's family; 'it's in the blood,' he says, and sometimes I cannot help laughing at his 'blood.' I asked him the other day how he was able to risk taking me into his house and entrusting me with his daughters' education when he knew nothing of my ancestors."

X

A VISIT TO CHARLESTON

Discouraged by the Peronneaus from traveling alone to Georgia on her summer vacation in 1854, Rosalie decided to remain in the Pineland, reading and catching up with her sewing, of which there seemed to be no end. The girls were invited by relatives to go visiting in Charleston, and Rosalie accompanied them as the guest of the Henry Peronneau family. On her return she had much to report to "beloved friends," 27 July 1854. "I spent 2½ weeks there . . . and would have been capable of enjoying more time there if the weather had not been so exceedingly hot. I was completely overcome the evening we set out, since I had been rushing about all day to get my things in order for the unexpected excursion. The thermometer has gone as high as 96° F, which is most unusual here; some of the Negroes had fallen ill of the intense heat so they had had to leave their work. Then they were allowed to rest during the hottest time of the day, here as well as on other plantations. In the city two people, both white, had died of sunstroke, and a couple of cases also had occurred among the blacks. Otherwise they endure the heat incomparably better than do the whites.

"I sensed at once a change in the air on our arrival in town. Here, the heat in the middle of the day is perhaps greater, since the tall pines surrounding us on all sides do not allow the air to circulate freely, but the atmosphere is drier than in town. Besides, we have the great advantage that the evenings, nights, and mornings are fresh and agreeable. But in town . . . morning, midday, or night are all alike, all hot, all humid. . . . During this time I learned to appreciate our summers, which even though they are short and often cool nevertheless provide us with so much pleasure and enjoyment, whereas the southerner complains about this time of year during which he lives only a half-life and longs for the winter. 'Providence has presumably intended that we sleep through the whole summer,' said a Charleston lady, whereas Tant Hammarsköld and I thought we have something bearlike in us and ought to go into hibernation all winter.

"My host and hostess were very amiable and attentive. . . . Mrs. Henry Peronneau is the liveliest, the most vivacious 'old lady' you have ever seen. The first one up in the morning and if one of the servants is sick, as has been the case now for a long while, she does the cleaning and dusting herself. When I came down at 6 o'clock she was in full swing with the duster." There were many parties to attend in the warm summer evenings, and Rosalie took careful note of the several kinds of refreshments that were served. "None of these refreshments are passed around but are carried in by the servants. The young ladies usually have a 'beau' (cavalier), whose duty it is to make himself as agreeable as possible, offer his arm to his fair one (the young ladies are called 'belles') if she wishes to stroll on the piazza, escort her to a chair or sofa if she prefers to sit, supply her with the refreshments she desires, fan her occasionally if it is warm, and finally, accompany her home. The older ladies, of whom relatively few are seen attending such parties, receive these attentions from the host and hostess. Strangely enough, the young ladies and the young gentlemen converse little or not at all with their friends but are almost exclusively devoted to their beau or belle and this right out in the open, no fault being found with it. It is quite usual to ask a young girl who has just come home from a party, 'Who was your beau for the evening?' If there is a lady there who is a stranger and has been somehow taken notice of, she usually does nothing other than sit still in the place she has first taken while the host, hostess, or others of her acquaintance present gentlemen to her who sit down next to her and converse for a while, one after the other. In the event there is a piano, those ladies who can play are selected for the sacrifice and entertain the company by taking their turn at it for a while. More often than not, however, the music is below average." (On the same subject Rosalie was later to write to her brother Axel, 13 August 1854, "Few take the trouble to listen to it, and among those who gather around the piano, most take more pleasure looking at the pianist's hands, if they happen to be pretty, than listening to the beauty of the melodies. To have the gentlemen play and sing—that is generally regarded as not suitable.") "The pleasures of society are based wholly on tête-à-tête and flirtation, for the young girls do not trouble to make conversation among themselves, and do not think they have had a good time unless they have had beaux. Dancing is not usual except at balls; games and diversions do not exist. The American usually converses more easily than does the Swede, and in the company of an interesting and entertaining cavalier the evening can pass pleasantly, but in the opposite case, it turns into a litany. An attempt was made at the Ravenels' to dance, but the heat was too great.

"One of the most interesting days in Charleston was the one I spent at the Museum. Mrs. Ravenel sent her carriage to fetch us, for it was a long way to walk in that terrible heat. Professor Holmes[1] greeted me at

1 Francis S. Holmes, Professor of Geology and Natural History in the College of

once with the greatest politeness, thanked me for the gifts of birds and eggs which he seemed to be very pleased with, showed me my old friend the owl as well as one of its brothers alive in a cage. He then asked me if I had seen their 'little pet,' by which he meant a sea monster, a devil fish, which had recently been caught in Charleston harbor. He then took me to a fenced-off place where this natural wonder was being kept. . . . It would have been impossible without assistance to decide if it belonged to mammals, birds, fish, or amphibians; it was like and unlike all of them. This strange fish, which has both wings and a tail, is 10 feet long, its tail looking like a snake, 6 feet long; the wings are 18 feet from tip to tip, with which it rushes at high speed through the water or throws itself high into the air. . . . The mouth measures 3 feet, but the throat is no wider than a fist. . . . It had been captured when its so-called horns had become entangled in a line belonging to a large schooner lying off Sullivan's Island. The other end of the line was fastened ashore, and the crew of the schooner noticed with astonishment that the ship was drifting. Not until after five hours' struggle and after the fish had tugged the ship about 300 yards did they succeed in capturing it.

"Professor Holmes promised to show me its teeth, but at that moment he was called away, and I was invited to enter Professor Gibbes's room to examine some experiments in natural philosophy that he had promised to show us. This is the same Gibbes[2] mentioned by Mlle. Bremer as the 'little lively astronomer,' an epithet which Mr. Peronneau thinks made Gibbes seethe a bit. He is shorter than I and extremely touchy and finicky, indescribably vivacious, with many gesticulations, is at home in the natural sciences and must be an excellent teacher; he showed us several experiments with the air pump, air gun, and in several other branches of science such as weighing air, counting the vibrations in a musical tone, gave us electromagnetic shocks, let us see a daguerreotype of the moon, and so on. I was very much interested in these experiments and wished only to see more of them. The instrument for counting the vibrations of various tones is the most precious thing and quite ingenious. . . . Our little professor was very eager to explain everything fully to us; meanwhile he panted and dried the perspiration on his forehead asking us now and then if we were tired. Before I leave Charleston I shall try to make another visit to the Museum.

Charleston; his collections formed a major part of the Museum when it was officially opened in January, 1852.

2 Lewis R. Gibbes, M.D., Professor of Mathematics and Natural Philosophy in the College of Charleston; called "the little lively astronomer" in *Homes of the New World* 1, 398.

"I have another nice day to tell you about which was spent on Sullivan's Island, just about the only summer resort which the city people have nearby. At 5 o'clock good Mrs. Peronneau came to awaken me, and at 7 we were aboard the little steamboat which was to take us to the island. On the way to the boat we went by the Market, where provisions are put on sale and where the gentlemen of the city go every morning to obtain supplies for the day.

"The company included Mrs. de Saussure with a couple of children, Clelia, Mary, and I. At the dock on Sullivan's Island we were met by old Mr. de Saussure, a little, portly, and prosperous-looking, exceedingly pleasant and genial old fellow, in whose carriage we went to his residence and were welcomed there by his wife and two daughters. After breakfast we sat on the piazza and I delighted in seeing and hearing the salt waves break against the fine sand of the shore just a few steps away from the house. Later we were invited to go out on 'the beach,' which at flood tide lies under water. Traveling across the white, fine-grained sand bar was especially pleasant, and we got down from the carriage to gather shells and seaweed which the waves had thrown up on the shore. Back at the house we were invited to go bathing, which we accepted with pleasure.

"One of the daughters let me borrow a bathing dress consisting of wide unmentionables and a jacket of red flannel, and a kind of coat of the same material to throw over my shoulders when descending into the water. Clelia and Mary received old bathing costumes of lesser elegance, and I assure you it was a droll sight to see us wandering off in this strange attire with old sunbonnets on our heads. In these bathing costumes the women can quite freely enjoy bathing in the sea without being concerned about onlookers; they are excellent for this purpose, although I should not feel myself inclined to be dressed in this manner or to go bathing with gentlemen, although this is said to be quite usual.

"It was glorious out in the water; it was thoroughly warm so that I did not feel one shiver when the first wave washed over me, and it was with difficulty that we could bring ourselves to leave the salty element after we had been in almost one hour. . . . Later it tasted marvelous to eat watermelons, apples, pineapples, bananas, fresh figs, raisins, and almonds, along with lemonade—doesn't it make your mouth water?

"Another time we were out sailing in a pretty little sloop, 'Undine,' which Mr. Parker and some other gentlemen owned, and saw the sea wall which has been built on the farthest point of the island as protection against the waves. We then sailed halfway around Fort Sumter, a new fortress built in an octagonal shape. . . . The entrance to Charleston seems to be well defended, and in addition there is Fort Johnson on a spit of land. The panorama of Charleston which we had before us was beautiful when lighted up in the evening glow and made so much more an impression on me as it was the first time in many a day that I had seen a sunset."

During these weeks in Charleston, Rosalie was also present for the celebration of the Fourth of July. "We set out early in the morning to watch from old Mr. de Saussure's house the parade, 'the soldiers,' which the natives regard as a magnificent show. The scene was animated, and great crowds of people, most of them colored, were swarming into the streets. Strangely enough, this jubilee of freedom is celebrated mostly by the slaves, who regard this day as their greatest holiday. They are out disporting themselves the whole day, and everywhere in the streets can be seen small tables covered with fruits, small cakes, ices, as well as coffee, tea, beer, and lemonade, presided over by colored canteen-keepers. Around them crowded Negroes and mulattoes of all shades and ages, all dressed up and tricked out in their finest. I have been astonished many times to see an elegant lady in a white lawn dress with trimmings, a little flower-bedecked hat, parasol, whose face closer up was seen to be black. They are generally much disposed to dress up gaudily, and it is not unusual to see them in muslin dresses, lawn, and barege.

"We had a good view from the beautiful, spacious piazza, but the soldiers were not much to look at. It was not a formed regiment, but only militia, resembling our civil guard though even less disciplined. The uniforms were tasteless, and the marching was done rather perfunctorily, scarcely two pairs of feet in step. . . . Our recruits would look down on them scornfully at the end of camp, but for all that they are real fighting men when there's need. The music, which was furnished only by darkeys, who have a far better ear than the Americans, was also second rate. The only ones I was interested in seeing were the Highlanders, who looked quite smart in their plaids, multicolored, checkered, going over the one shoulder and tied under the arm, and also their tall hats. Finally there were the so-called ragamuffins . . . made up of that part of the militia who do not want to don uniforms. They did look very amusing with hats— black, gray, or straw—caps of various shapes, and coats of various colors. All the officers were mounted, and as the day was hot, they were all well pleased when the spectacle came to an end. After the morning's festivities, the women withdrew each to her own affairs and left the field to the coloreds and the blacks. who took full advantage of it.

"The fashionable world did not begin to bestir itself until evening, when a show of fireworks was shot up from a vessel alongside the Battery. I really enjoyed the evening's entertainment. It was all new to me, and I took great pleasure in seeing the blue vault of heaven spangled with sparkling stars, and the clear mirror of water reflecting the heavenly lights. A diversified group of people had come there, unlike those seen at home made up only of well, indeed elegantly dressed persons listening to relatively good music . . . and also with beautiful fireworks. At times a bluish snake unwound itself hissing over our heads and came down sometimes like beautiful stars in various colors, sometimes like a glowing rain of fire. In addition there were suns, stars, wheels of fire, a sea battle, and finally freedom's temple set in diamonds of fire with Washington's name in the middle. . . . But how quiet this crowd of people was, no shoving, not one obstreperous word, yet they were well over a thousand, and if a woman came near a bench or a good spot occupied by a gentleman, he left his place at once to offer it to her. Such attentiveness and respect for women are a trait which the old world could well learn from the new. Yet another aspect of the good side of Charleston is to be mentioned—that is, that I never feel the least fear of being insulted or frightened by waterside roughs of either the upper or lower classes.

"I was once witness to the passing of a couple of processions that were in their way new to me. The first was a Negro funeral, which is always carried out with great pomp. The hearse comes first, then several couples in mourning, a man and a woman arm in arm, then the men with crape tied around their hats and with the ends two ells long, the women in black dresses and black veils hanging down from each side of the hat; after them came several couples in less deep mourning, the women in straw hats with black bands, white dresses and black sashes, the black gentlemen in white vests mixed in toward the end with one or another colored. But I cannot deny that some of the black beauties showed up very amusingly as they came mincing along pleased with themselves and taking peacock steps. Most of them did not look deeply stricken by grief. The night between the death and the burial the deceased's friends sit around the body together and sing hymns.

"The other funeral was even more remarkable and was that of an Irishman who in a quarrel that had led to fighting had received from the American nine knife wounds, of which three were fatal. I was out one morning on King Street to do some shopping when I began to hear music, which on closer inspection was found to originate in a corps of black musicians following a platoon of soldiers; after them came a squad of soldiers, then a huge hearse, drawn by two pairs of white horses. Then followed several carriages with ladies, then some Negroes, and finally a procession of men walking two by two, which I thought would never come to an end. Some had long black crape hanging around the hats;

others, however, were attired in bright colors; there were some curious physiognomies there, but most of them looked stalwart and not to be fooled with. After this enormous procession, which was said to consist of 700 persons, all Irishmen, there followed all sorts of vehicles, most of them of an antique appearance, fully occupied by ladies, and finally came some men on horseback. The number of carriages came to 40. It is said that the Irish wanted to use this occasion to display a corps in order to let people see how strong they are numerically.

"King Street, along which all the lower stories consist of shops, is three miles long from the Battery where it begins until it turns into a country road. Swarms of ladies begin to be out on it around 6 o'clock, some on foot, some in carriages, one or another on horseback. Nearly all of them are dressed as though for a ball in bright silk dresses, wool and silk barege, lawn and muslin dresses and carrying fans; the ladies who ride are mostly bareheaded. The ones walking are sometimes out shopping, but mostly to make visits and to see people, toilets, and to meet friends on King Street. Carriage after carriage rolls up King Street, then onto the plank road out to the highway which has one side designated for the outward bound, the other for those returning. I was out a few times with a Tant, enjoying myself looking at le beau monde and inhaling plenty of dust. One time we traveled as far as Magnolia Cemetery. . . . On the way home we drove through King Street, it was late and all the gas lights were lighted, which is always a beautiful prospect. The many ice cream shops look particularly alluring with their little pavilions for two or three persons, entwined in vines, and there is a fountain in the middle of one of them. Women can go there, alone or in company, any hour of the day, and refresh themselves with different kinds of ice cream and fruit for 6¼ cents. Everywhere when you are out in the evening or even at home ice cream is put out on the table. Even on the streets ice cream is carried around for sale, the hawkers shouting 'ice cream' in long drawn-out calls. Several kinds of things to be eaten are sold in this manner; the first thing I heard in the morning was 'watermillions' (the Negroes' pronunciation of 'watermelons') in a recitative; so too with chickens, fresh eggs, fresh butter, okra (a vegetable much in demand from which is prepared a soup with the addition of tomatoes which the South Carolinians eat all summer), green corn, tomatoes, and mullets (a kind of fish). The watermelons are in general a favorite fruit, and how many thousands are eaten daily in Charleston it would be impossible to say. Carts loaded with them cross all the streets of the city, the many fruit stores are filled with them, and at the Market they were beyond counting. . . .

"Figs grow in abundance in Charleston, several kinds, very prolific, three harvests a year. But peaches, the marvelous peaches, we shall have to do without this year for they were almost totally damaged by frost. The Swedish consul, however, had the civility to send a darkey with a tray covered with a white napkin and lo! in a crystal bowl had been placed on their leaves some large, beautiful peaches, a delight to sight, smell, and taste, and on them a charming little note to 'Miss Russe.' "

It had still remained uncertain whether any of Rosalie's brothers would try their luck in America. Axel found employment with the newly started railroad construction in Sweden, but then to Rosalie's surprise she had learned that the work might have to be halted for financial reasons, in which case Axel might perhaps come to America after all. She wrote to him 13 August 1854: "How unfortunate it would be both for the good of the country and for the sake of those who have been employed at the great enterprise if the railroad construction should come to a standstill after having finally been started after lengthy discussions. That no country can be compared to the United States in this field is incontestable, and there still is long-term work to be done. A railroad is to be built between Charleston and Savannah, for which proposals were made and measurements taken last winter. Another larger railroad called 'the northeast' is, if I am not mistaken, to provide more direct communication between the northern and southern states, and a huge project which is talked about is a railroad to the Pacific. You see then that there is no lack of work here in your specialty, nor do I think a competent engineer would find it difficult to get work. . . .

"I was glad to hear that they have finally got the electric telegraph at home—this invention, though simple, may be regarded as a marvel. From a practical point of view I think that inventions which lead to savings in time and space, which exert an influence on mechanical and mercantile interests, have permitted England and America to do more for our times than any other nation. They are behind in the arts and sciences.

"One looks in vain here for the spirit of poetry which hovers over 'the old countries' and manifests itself in monuments from the prehistoric past, in traditions and legends, in the songs of the people and even in its temperament. For us Europeans, the poetical elements in America consist of the Indians and the primeval forests. The natives despise the former and are indifferent to the latter. A spirit of business pervades this nation made up of so many heterogeneous components."

Questions from home regarding Fredrika Bremer's *Homes of the New World* evoked comment from Rosalie in a letter to her father, 18 September 1854, on her reading and on her impressions so far of Miss Bremer's book. "You mention that the third part of Fredrika Bremer's 'Homes' has now appeared in Sweden, and that you are reading it. Over here the whole book came out at one time in two parts, but I have not yet finished Part Two. Take away the time needed for lessons, music practice, letter writing, mending, and sewing, and there is not much left over for reading. . . . I have, besides, a full month's reading in 'Harper's Magazine,' which contains many articles on all possible subjects that are worth reading. . . . For more than a year it has carried Abbot's history of Napoleon, a quite interesting and entertaining work, though it is said to have greater value as 'a work of fiction' than as history. Another big work being published there is 'The Newcomes, Memories of a Most Respectable Family': it is cleverly written and contains a good deal of satire, as is the wont of the author, Thackeray. . . . When I come home I am going to have 'Harper's.' Another magazine is the 'London Quarterly Review,' which is on a higher level with regard to both science and literature. I have read in it an article about magnetism, somnambulism, and table moving, so extremely well written and enlightening that it was a real pleasure to read it; since it explained for me several phenomena about which I had thought many times and wondered greatly whether they should be believed or doubted, it possessed double interest for me.

"I have digressed completely from my subject, which was Mlle. Bremer's book. . . . Her 'Homes' is, as I have mentioned, not appreciated here, and not particularly pretty epithets have been applied to the author: that she has been a spy, has acted shamelessly, and so on. She is too much an abolitionist to think of retaining any friends in 'the South' after the publication of her book. It is impossible to imagine the bitterness and hatred between the North and South, between slave owners and abolitionists; it is a case of fist in the face, knife to the throat—if not in actuality, then in the feeling between the parties. The Indian Territory lying west of the slave state Missouri is now to be organized, if I am not mistaken, into two new territories, Nebraska and Kansas. Immigration is open to all, and time and the people who settle there are to determine if these territories are to be taken into the Union as free or as slave states. The controversy is a stubborn one, for neither side will yield a hairsbreadth. In the northern states societies are formed to promote emigration from there and through colonization of the country by abolitionists to prepare it to become a free state. On the other hand, the southern states rise up—and especially the neighboring states, which do not care to have a free neighbor—and form societies for a purpose contrary to that of the northern states and declare at public meetings that they will mutually protect and defend each other's rights and property whether consisting of land or slaves, that they do not intend to interfere with the rights of others but neither will they permit invasions of their own, but will defend them if necessary to the last drop of blood. In consequence of this rivalry between conflicting interests the new territories probably will be populated unbelievably fast. I copy out here a piece from a newspaper to illustrate southern thinking on the slave question: 'God has ordained and approved slavery, nature has required and made it necessary, mankind has supported it. We do not need to seek to be more righteous than God, more just than nature, wiser than the experience of centuries.'

"I mentioned that Mlle. Bremer's book does not have and cannot have admirers in the South, but even in the northern states it has reduced her popularity, and the reason for that is the publicity she has given those homes where she had been received with such good will, the judgments and the descriptions she has given of private individuals, at times extravagantly flattering, at times poking fun a little, in both cases unpleasant for the individuals. This behavior of hers is regarded as a breach of hospitality and in the future will close American homes and hearts to foreigners, especially of the literary sort.

"I find much of interest in her book, but several mistakes, much exaggeration, and too much 'I.' The rich materials she obtained in America could have been better used, to the advantage of both the author and the public."

To her father on 29 July 1854 Rosalie passed what appears to have been her final judgment on Miss Bremer's book: "It is unbecoming to make public a private correspondence which ought in any case not to have been published by the author herself. It seems to me as though the words of the song could be applied to this matter also: 'Is there any mortal here on earth, who is not a bit of a charlatan?' She brings so much into her letters that has nothing to do with the subject, so much that seems to be there to show off her knowledge and philosophical bent of mind, so many private matters that cannot be of interest to the public at large. . . . Perhaps I judge incorrectly or am mistaken, perhaps the author of these letters is more profound than it is within my ability to comprehend. I am, however, convinced that she means well and nobly although I do not care for <u>all</u> her views on the question of woman's liberation."

XI

TRAVEL PLANS

In a letter to her father dated 18 September 1854 Rosalie explained some of the difficulties complicating her plans for travel after leaving Charleston. She was not to be thought lacking in determination, she insisted, for had she not already shown, she asked, that once having made up her mind she was not easily deterred from carrying out her ideas? "However, Mr. Peronneau and his friends have already begun to represent to me the disagreeableness and indeed the perils for a woman undertaking such a tour as I have laid out without a protector. Such remarks make me unhappy, for I see that I cannot undertake my journey without upsetting thereby the prejudices of a family I love and respect, but they cannot compel me to depart from the purpose I have determined upon. Here is one of the many examples of the power of prejudice in the promised land of freedom, and I could cite many more. Mrs. Peronneau became quite displeased with me because, retaining my old custom of going on solitary walks when I can find no one to accompany me, I set out on little excursions on my own in the Pineland where scarcely anyone other than the residents was to be seen. She pretended that she was afraid that someone would give me offense, but I am afraid that the true reason was that it is not thought suitable for a woman to go walking alone. At home neither propriety nor fear of giving offense imposed such a restriction on my wishes; I could wander about freely there any time of the day.

"You chided me for having given up my trip to Georgia, Papa. But you little know what it is to be dependent on others. . . . If the journey could have been undertaken direct by railway, I would not have hesitated; but not only would I have had to change trains, but I would have had to travel 60 miles in a diligence on unmarked roads. The Peronneaus would have considered this to be utterly outlandish, and if in spite of their protests I had defied all the rules of propriety, how would I have been received by their relatives living there, and how by them themselves on my return? Papa dear, it is not so easy after all for a woman to disregard the opinions of others, especially when she is not independent; and so long as I am thought of as a member of another family, I must conduct myself in accordance with their prejudices and views. When I become my own master,

I shall do what I please and I shall then travel alone if I cannot find anyone to come with me." In a later letter to her father, 29 October 1854, Rosalie was still feeling obliged to defend her situation. "Do not suppose, however, that I will be given such help and be as petted as was Mlle. Bremer—there's a great difference between us! How can you even think of comparing my travels with hers? She, a widely known, widely read and respected author with her name serving as a letter of introduction wherever she might go, and I, a completely obscure person whose existence is known only on the small plot of earth where I happen to be. I should indeed have fairly exaggerated expectations if I were to look for the same show of friendliness and attention which fell to Miss Bremer's lot—and so romantic an idea as that I might meet people who would invite me to travel or stay with them at no cost has never gained a hold in my mind. . . . When Miss Bremer arrived anywhere, she was greeted with friendly invitations to enter congenial homes and families, but when Miss Roos appears, she will have to be grateful if some kindly person directs her to a decent hotel, and it is fairly certain that no steamboat captains or railroad companies will send her complimentary tickets.

"However, this does not affect my travel plans, for I must make my way home, and to leave America without having seen more than South Carolina seems quite unthinkable. Courageously, and trusting in God's protection, I shall therefore set out and let people talk as much as they like, but on no account do I delude myself with any sanguine notions as to the ease and pleasure of traveling alone but prepare myself for the difficulties to be encountered, of which the greatest almost seems to me to be to calculate the costs of travel so that my funds will not be exhausted before I have again set foot on Swedish soil. I would like very much to go to Cuba. In New Orleans I will get help and support from the members of the Logan family living there. . . .

"The senatorial elections have now come to an end, and many intrigues, dollars, and large quantities of whisky have figured in the attempt to persuade the voters of the merits of the various candidates. It has been rather enjoyable listening to the political discussions between Mr. Peronneau, the monarchical-minded republican, and Mr. Niemann, the republican Prussian. Several of Mr. Peronneau's friends who were candidates for the Senate have missed out, and Peronneau claims that there is more honor in not being elected than in being elected. In Charleston a Jew succeeded in securing so large a plurality of votes that he was elected, but it is also said that the business cost him $25,000. A nice little fortune for an election!"

On 23 September 1854, in one of her lengthy letters addressed to "all my dear ones," Rosalie described the effects of a storm that had evidently reached hurricane force: "This time my letter will not contain anything very cheerful, for death and destruction are reported from every quarter in the United States. Cholera is raging in the northern and middle states, yellow fever in the southern, and the coastal plains of Carolina and Georgia have been visited by a storm the likes of which have not been known for half a century and which destroyed in a couple of days the expectations of many plantation owners for a good harvest. Here in the Pineland where the buildings are surrounded by dense woods, we seldom feel any breeze, but on Thursday the 7th of September we were favored the whole day with a brisk wind, quite welcome in the heat we had been experiencing. Toward evening it grew stronger, threatening black clouds covered the sky, which was crisscrossed by brilliant flashes of lightning while the thunder testified in majestic tones to the might of the Creator. Mr. Parker, who arrived at about 8 o'clock, was completely covered with dust which had swirled in eddies all about him. The wild spirit of the storm howled and grew all the more violent, and the tall pines swayed like reeds and moaned under the mighty beating of its wings, which uprooted a pine here, snapped off an oak there, and sent showers of cones and needles onto the ground. I was awakened by the awful noise which together with the dazzling lightning kept me awake the whole night. The doors shook, and their rattling blended in with the mighty concert. The day dawned but the storm continued unabated, and we now saw evidence of the night's destruction in several trees that had fallen around us. So it continued all of Friday and all the following night, and although the wind was not again so fierce, the bad weather continued with thunder, lightning, and rain which lasted until Sunday morning.

"On Saturday the mail did not come since the ferry across the Ashley could not operate. In addition, all communication was blocked by the washing away of bridges and the barricades of fallen trees. Dr. Logan, who had been prevented for three days from visiting his patients, came riding in on Sunday and described conditions in the city: the eastern part of the Battery is completely destroyed. Within a few minutes the embankment was smashed to pieces by the monstrous waves which then rushed up into the streets, into which the smaller steamships and vessels were also driven. The water made its way into several houses and cellars, houses were blown down, numerous trees suffered the same fate, roofs were torn off churches and dwellings, and the greatest anxiety was felt by those who had relatives and friends on Sullivan's Island, for it was feared that it would be completely laid waste by the storm. Its inhabitants, however, escaped with nothing worse than a bad fright and the loss of 16 to 20 houses.

"When Mr. Peronneau arrived at his plantation on Saturday, he found his beautiful, partly harvested rice crop floating about in the flooded fields. It was not until Tuesday's post that more detailed information could be obtained of the damage done by the storm. The largest part was due to flooding, for no one remembers having seen the waters rise so high before. The rice crop this year had seemed unusually promising, but more than half is thought to have been destroyed, and what remains has been more or less damaged. The plantations along the Savannah River have suffered unbelievably. . . . The cotton crop has also been partly damaged. Mr. Peronneau figures that he has lost three-quarters of his particularly fine crop. . . . They have labored desperately to gather up out of the water what had been cut, even at times during the night by torchlight. Mr. Peronneau left the house in the mornings at 7, came back at 8 or 9 in the evenings without having tasted a bite to eat during the day and wet above his knees from wading in the water. Despite all the work and haste, the rice began to sprout in the stalks because the weather turned very hot, and there then followed several days of steady rain which filled the bog lying beyond his fields so that the water began to break through the earthen dikes on that side also. New cause for anxiety and worry. It was exactly like being in an entrenchment surrounded by enemies who continually batter the ramparts. One time Mr. Peronneau did not come home until between 2 and 3 in the night. Next to such perseverance our estimable tillers of the soil have to fall back into the shadows. And when he comes home in the evening he does not seem at all tired but can sit up until midnight if he has someone to talk to. In the middle of all this the rice birds have now arrived, those little plunderers which I mentioned last year, and since he cannot spare any workers to shoot them, he has been obliged to give up as lost to them 17 acres of the rice that was planted last, the grains of which have not yet hardened but contain only the so-called rice milk, which the feathered freebooters regard as a delicacy. Nor have I ever heard Mr. Peronneau utter a word of complaint or discontent. He says only: 'It's hard to see one's work disappear so in a few days, but it is my own fault, for if I had brought in the rice that had been stacked, I would have been spared a large part of this loss.'

"Savannah has been stricken for a long time with yellow fever, which has wreaked cruel havoc there,—we receive melancholy reports daily: several physicians have fallen victim to the epidemic, a large portion of the population has fled, several hotels have closed, and all the stores have ceased doing business. The incidence of disease has been so great among the bakers that there was no bread to be had in Savannah, but it had to be obtained in Charleston, and although the sickness there has not been virulent, it is nevertheless enough to arouse concern and anxiety. The death toll varies between 19 and 26 daily.

"Dr. de Saussure's boys hovered between life and death; several of the Peronneau family's friends have lost children. Among my fellow countrymen in the city I do not know how matters stand other than that I have seen the name of the youngest Myhrman listed among the dead. . . . On Friday there were services in all the churches of the city for a day of penance and prayer, when the offerings were made in behalf of the needy. From the other states there are similarly gloomy reports coming in as to the cholera, which is also spreading death and sorrow among the thousands.

"So as not to have you suppose we do not share in the prevailing sickness, we have caught some colds to remind us that we too are frail mortals. Mr. Peronneau doses the sick with calomel, castor oil, and quinine, and I chaff him by saying that I am less afraid of being sick than of being 'doctored.' "

The time was soon approaching for Rosalie to set out on her long journey home when she wrote to her father from "Dungannon" 27 November 1854: "I am now thinking seriously of the great voyage across the sea to the Northland—to the Northland! The beginning of my life as a chevalière errante next year will occur three weeks from now, when I decamp here and visit my friends in North Carolina. My visit with them will probably not extend beyond the end of February, when I return to Charleston. You do not seem to care for my Cuba plans which nevertheless comprise one of my most cherished ideas and which I would find difficult to give up. There is no danger of yellow fever at the time of year when my visit would take place, for that sickness dies out after the first frost. . . . Nor have there been any disturbances reported from that island, but in the event that they might break out, all my travel plans would of themselves come of course to nothing. It is my hope and my effort now to be able to obtain a letter of introduction to some Christian person there. The Swedish consul in Charleston did not know if a similar official would have been assigned to Havana. I suppose, however, that the Swedish government has a consul in a city of that importance and wonder if you couldn't obtain for me an introduction to the aforesaid personage. The pleasantest though not the cheapest way of getting to New Orleans is via Cuba."

Rosalie's travel plans had already given rise of course to considerable concern about her clothes, but she was determined to ply her needle with great diligence during her visit with the Hammarskölds. In a letter to her mother 25 September 1854 she wrote: "Papa says, 'If you have sufficient funds, it is easy enough to get all you need without having to carry it with you.' Good and true, but as that will not be my situation, I shall have to take with me what I need in order to avoid as much as possible outlays for my wardrobe. . . . I want to take with me as few clothes as possible, but we women unfortunately cannot manage to get along with as few garments as gentlemen do, especially when one must always appear well dressed. Here more than anywhere the old saying applies, 'The apparel oft proclaims the man.'. . . .

"In New Orleans there is even greater luxury, and all the ladies have their hairdressers. The Hammarskölds lived there for two years. Emilie has told how poor they were when they first went there, but nonetheless had to live in one of the most expensive hotels in order to become known and to have audiences at the concerts she gave; Hjalmar used to dress her hair for her as he had seen how the other ladies had theirs dressed.

"I have a lot to do now and spur on the girls' studies as much as possible . . . and will continue with this until the 18th of December, after which I shall barely have time to make some purchases in Charleston. I shall not have time to visit Hulda until the return journey. She is very much in the good graces of the Legarés, who do not wish by any means to let her go but try to persuade her that her health will not tolerate a more northerly climate. She is not so robust and red cheeked as she was at Limestone, has also become very nervous and has almost entirely withdrawn from intercourse with her countrymen. We write to each other though not often, and her letters are usually short and hurried. She has a very good salary at Orangeburg, $700, unusual even here. Franz gets the same, but he feels less content, for he is of that sort who are seldom satisfied with their lot and circumstances.

"Mr. Peronneau was very anxious to get a Swedish governess to succeed me and bade me write and ask you to obtain one, but I said that I did not personally know anyone I could recommend. He would provide for the voyage here and also the return home if they were not to be paid for in cash, but after further consultation with his wife, he has abandoned this idea. When I return from North Carolina I shall probably stay with them for 2 to 3 weeks during which time the girls can have lessons from me."

From Spring Hill, North Carolina, Rosalie was able to write, 18 January 1855, that the visit that had long been planned for her at the

Parker plantation, "Old Town,"[1] had finally taken place. "I was invited there in order to see the orange trees with their treasure of golden fruit. The visit had been postponed time and again, because the bridge on the road was to be repaired, the horses were halt, lame, or at work; and I had finally given up every hope of getting there when Mr. Peronneau offered me and Clelia the chance of going if we would be willing to content ourselves with a pair of mules to pull the wagon. We agreed, but it was the most miserable journey I have ever made, for the mules refused to move and would only budge a few steps, and in order to hasten them along it was necessary to use a whip constantly. In the first place I am no friend of such behavior, and in the second, it is the mule's nature to be extremely stubborn when it turns obstinate. Our driver made full use of the whip he brought with him on the poor animals and also of several heavy switches which he cut along the way. . . . It made my heart ache to see the poor animals treated thus, and every now and then I would enter a plea for them, but was told in reply that they did not feel it. We finally arrived after 4 to 5 hours (14 miles), and were cordially received by our host."

On the way to the orange grove Rosalie passed the "cotton house" and was able to acquaint herself with the processing of cotton before it was packed into bales. The only machines which lightened the work were a row of cotton gins used to separate the seed from the cotton. "A man stands at each of these machines and while he works the treadle, he feeds the cotton over the rollers, which as they turn pull it down into a drawer in the back. It is a quite simple but efficient machine for its purpose, about three feet wide, and tall enough so that a man can stand comfortably and feed the cotton over the rollers. Before it was invented, the seed had to be removed by hand, which was a tremendous job since the seed is tightly entangled in the wool. A plantation owner expressed his dissatisfaction with this one time in the presence of his son's tutor, who had a good head for mechanics, and asked him if he could not hit upon some easier way of cleaning the cotton. With the help of a couple of knitting needles he assembled a little model machine which was the beginning of the now widely used cotton gin. . . . The cotton that I saw was long, so-called sea-island cotton, a far better and finer grade than we have at home. . . .

1 The site of the original English settlement in 1670 on the southwest side of the Ashley River; the government moved ten years later across the river to Oyster Point and laid out what became Charles Town, the present city of Charleston. "Old Town" fell into decay and passed through many hands into the possession of Alexander Perronneau, Jr., and eventually of William Parker at the time of Rosalie's visit. See Henry A. M. Smith, "Old Charles Town and Its Vicinity," *South Carolina Historical and Genealogical Magazine* 16 (1915), 1–15, 49–67.

"I return now to the orange trees, in which I took particular delight. On a smooth lawn near the banks of the river stood a number of these evergreen trees, but only a few of them were still resplendent with their shining fruit. The unusually severe cold weather that occurred in the beginning of December had obliged Mr. Parker to strip the trees of the largest part of the fruit and he had only left some trees so that I might get to see them. The beautiful oranges often grow tightly together in large clusters, but among the trees that had been stripped had been a branch with 60 fruits which Mr. Parker had sent as a present to a friend. . . . Mr. Parker had picked 8000 oranges, and before we set out on the way home we were in a storeroom where there were 4000 and we ate as many as we had room for.

"After dinner we started off on the way home, and it was with no little rejoicing that I saw Mr. Parker's horses and wagon standing before the door, hence pleasanter prospects for the homeward journey. Poor donkeys, they had to carry home instead a bag of oysters and another of oranges to 'Dungannon.'

"Back home, I found my room had been decorated with leaves, a wreath placed on Papa's portrait, and candles lighted in honor of my birthday. . . . Mary was deeply distressed that she had not been able to get eggs for a birthday cake. Mrs. Peronneau, however, had had rice pudding prepared for me, and the cake, decorated with moss, heads of rice, and cedar appeared a few days later.

"The 18th of December had been fixed for my departure, but although I worked—like a slave is to put it too mildly, for they surely never overwork themselves—but until my strength failed me and Mrs. Peronneau forced me to rest a while, I did not manage to be ready in the morning as I had wanted. Mama, just imagine that on the same day that I had decided to set aside for packing, I still had the whole room at 1 o'clock inundated with dried flowers! But Eliza and Anna kindly helped me get the herbarium in order." This and several other things were to be sent to Sweden in care of Captain Rydin, who had taken responsibility for earlier shipments to and from America in Rosalie's behalf.

"On Thursday morning Mr. Logan accompanied me to the railroad, and although the day was cold, I was so well provided for that I felt no discomfort from the cold. To keep my feet warm during the journey Mr. Peronneau had made me a present of a little hassock of sheet iron provided with holes as in a grater; inside was placed a pan with glowing coals and thus it offered a pleasant warmth. . . . To my dismay the train schedule had been revised . . . so that I was not to arrive at Charlotte until 1 o'clock at night. At Columbia Hjalmar helped me on board and entrusted me to the care of the conductor in case no one would have come to meet me in Charlotte. The journey, however, turned out to be pleasanter than I had dared hope. I read as long as I could see, conversed a while with some women who came and sat with me and asked a number of questions about Sweden, and also with the engineer, who nevertheless struck me as being a little 'green' though of a kindly disposition. I had been a little afraid of traveling on the railroad at night, for besides the unpleasantness of it for women as well as the greater danger to which one is exposed in the dark, a gentleman had recently been robbed of $6000 in the course of a night-time journey. While he sat dozing a couple of rascals had cleverly got him to breathe chloroform and could then do with him what they pleased. But now we proceeded without incident. No one had come to meet me, but the engineer secured space in an omnibus for me and my things, and on my arrival at the hotel the innkeeper came to meet me asking if I were Miss Roos, showed me to a room, and said that he had been commissioned by Mr. Hammarsköld to secure a wagon for me. The next day I did get the wagon and a well-mannered driver. Since the road was laid with planks and the horses were strong and good natured, everything went well at first, but unfortunately my driver did not know the way, and the persons we asked were just as ignorant. We ended up taking the wrong road and when we at last realized it, we were to look for a short cut to get back to the right road, but this short cut was more dreadful than any road I have traveled on with Papa, for at times it looked as though we would be going straight up the mountain and at other times as though we were about to plunge into an abyss. At every moment I thought that the wagon and harness would break in two or the horses stumble and fall, and it was with a profound sense of happiness and gratitude that I once again found myself on the plank road. But however far we continued on it, the mystery remained where we were to turn off. No dwellings could be seen, not a person did we meet. . . . But at last we saw a cottage in a valley and my driver went there to make inquiries and received the desired information, and by sunset we drove into the yard at Spring Hill. . . .

"During the Christmas holiday we had summer weather so that on Christmas Day we sat out on the piazza to drink our coffee. The thermometer registered 20° C.

"There is a water shortage here, for there has scarcely been any rain since September. Although the river is rather broad, there is so little water in it that the forge has hardly operated half the time. This means a big loss for Hammarsköld, for when all goes well he makes a profit of $100 from the forge every week; now there is probably very little left over after taking into account the high wages. Otherwise the forge operates both day and night and Hammarsköld and Carl are sometimes down there until 1 and 2 at night, sometimes going there at 3 or 4 in the morning. They are indeed industrious, energetic, and economical, but they have encountered unbelievable reverses since their arrival in America. Besides the forge they sell flour and have a store here. All the buildings belonging to the forge were swept away by floods in the fall a year ago so that Hammarsköld had the present ones constructed besides having a saw built in order to be able to saw some timber. The mill is also here and since it is quite good, wheat is purchased and is later sold as flour, but now there is no wheat to be had. The wages are not inconsiderable; the Negroes are paid between $10 and $12 a month, the white workers' daily wage varies between 50 cents and $1.50. A number of draught animals are also needed, and Hammarsköld has 20 horses and donkeys of his own which are in constant use for transporting ore, coal, iron, wheat, and flour. The gold mine was not especially profitable; expenses came to over $150 and the gold that was found amounted to less than $50. Gold is said to be present everywhere, but in such small quantities as not to warrant the cost of labor. . . .

"I mustn't forget to tell you about the Masons' dance in Lincolnton! An invitation was waiting for me when I arrived, and I had scarcely time to get myself ready to ride to it in company with Heddie and Carl. . . . I was a little taken aback when I made my entrance, for it did not precisely correspond to my expectations. The room was scarcely as large as Lundsbrunn's salon, and, like it, had pillars the length of the room. It was full of people; to judge by their dress and deportment, the illumination and the music, it seemed to me as though I had come to a big country wedding. The furniture consisted of some wooden chairs and wooden benches painted green; the music, of a fiddle, a triangle, and a tambourine. All the musicians were Negroes, and the violin player shouted out in a loud voice the figures which were to be danced. His hoarse voice, accompanied by his screeching violin, the jingling of the tambourine, and the tinkling of the triangle, was hardly a delight to the ears. The dances consisted only of cotillions. Most of the men wore coats, colored neckerchiefs, and vests; some were with and others without gloves. Most of the ladies wore white dresses and colored berets; they were all badly and tastelessly dressed! Since we arrived a little late, there were no other places than near the door which opened out to the street, and next to it was a window, also open, which served as a framework for a couple of dozen black, grinning physiognomies. I therefore preferred dancing to being observed and accepted the invitations I received. Some of my partners looked quite comical. There were no refreshments to be had other than water, but between 10 and 11 a supper was ready. It was, however, set out at another place a good distance from the dance hall so that we had to ride to get to it. My last dancing partner, a big fat peony-red gentleman, asked if he might not escort me to the supper. In for a penny, in for a pound, and consequently I thought I ought to say yes, but I must admit I felt a little frightened by my unknown knight who looked as though he were a devotee of Bacchus, and when we passed Carl, I whispered to him, 'Dear Carl, don't desert me!'

"I was taken by my 'beau' in a buggy hitched up to two mules to the house where the supper was to be served. We were the first ones there; to my joy Heddie and Carl followed soon after. The supper was quite elegant with much food, tea and coffee, splendid cakes and pies, syllabub, custard, and jellies, but no liquor. After the gentlemen had fed their ladies, they led them into another room and then did justice themselves to the repast. After supper we drove back and the dance was resumed, but after a couple of dances, we left to make our way home."

To her father Rosalie wrote the next day, 19 January 1855, that she had never felt happier and more carefree than she did then. She was obviously enjoying her respite from responsibilities at Charleston, and with her friends she could lower her guard and speak her mind about the differences in manners and customs to which she had tried with less than perfect success to accommodate herself in America. In the letter to her father she tried to achieve a balanced view of one of the most troubling subjects in their correspondence; slavery she saw on the one hand as a moral wrong harmful to slave and owner alike, on the other as the Peronneaus and many others in their class regarded it, as an "economic necessity" mitigated by humane custom among native-born southerners. "I am in agreement with what you say about slavery, for although I have never seen any mistreatment of slaves and am <u>entirely</u> convinced that <u>many</u> of them are better off than their poor white brothers, there is something in the idea itself that is so repugnant that I can never reconcile myself to it. And I am sorry not only for the slaves but also for the owners, for various reasons. For immigrants this institution is a greater evil than can be imagined. In old native-born families where the slaves are handed down from father to son and the black and white children grow up together, a real affection arises between masters and servants, and the latter regard themselves as members of the former's family, and thereby provide superb examples of faithful retainers, who scarcely exist at home other than in novels. For immigrants, the situation is otherwise. If they hire white servants, they are lazy, insolent, and expect something better than waiting at table. Hire or buy blacks, they usually are the poorest, those whom the owners wanted to be rid of."

In the same letter Rosalie took up once more her travel plans. "I have not yet come to any definite decision about traveling to Cuba, but find it impossible to get it out of my head and many have urged me to go. There are two departures a month from Charleston by the steamship 'Isabel,' which runs between New York and Havana and puts in at Charleston. Mr. Parker, who knows the captain of the 'Isabel,' said that he did not know any captain into whose care he would willingly leave a woman with greater confidence. The only stumbling block is cost, as much of the voyage as of expenses there, for I know that it will be an expensive place— but, but it is also difficult to be so near this crown jewel of Spain, this earthly paradise, and not to take a peek in. I shall try to get as much information as possible and then do my level best to arrange matters—to compute expenses for everything is and will be my most perplexing question. . . .

"However, may I ask you, Papa, for a letter of credit on some bank in London to be used in case of need there? Hammarsköld has urged me to do this, for London is a dangerous place in many respects; even if one arrives there with a well-filled purse, there are a thousand ways of making off with it from an inexperienced traveler, and to find oneself in London without money, without a protector, would be, to say the least, a vexing situation. On the other hand, the worth of a letter of credit is null and void unless I have signed my name to it . . . and I do not propose to make use of it if I am not obliged by necessity, for I would very much prefer to assume the cost of my travels myself. But if I were obliged to use the credit, I ask that I may look on it as a loan."

Her long Christmas holiday with the Hammarskölds was over; Rosalie returned to "Dungannon" and on 16 March 1855 wrote to her father of the fires that had been raging in the area. "Everywhere people complain of being short of money; another subject for worry is the continuing drought. Much damage has been caused this spring by fire—for it is customary here to set fire to the woods in the spring to burn up leaves, dry twigs, and so-called underwood in order to secure better grazing for the animals. This custom, an appalling one in my view, was followed again this year, but because of the lengthy drought and much wind, the fire has caught hold all round in a terrible way. Several weeks ago we were surrounded by fires and shrouded in a quite unpleasant atmosphere of smoke which concealed all but the closest objects, dried our throats, and made our eyes water. We suffered nothing worse and have cause to be grateful, for at other places they have not been so fortunate. Several houses have burned down, some with all their contents, barns, cotton storerooms, machines, railroads, trains loaded with cotton and other goods; passenger trains have been delayed and derailed, and fences, firewood, and animals the victims of the flames. According to a letter from Tant Hammarsköld, a fire had been raging there too, so that they were almost afraid of losing not only several thousand cords of split firewood, but the forge and the dwelling houses were also in danger of going up in flames. They succeeded in saving most of it. . . . A small town up there is said to have burned completely down, and in many places people have been in danger of their lives. At one place the fire had spread so rapidly that 70 to 90 hogs had been burned in the woods. From the hill at Spring Hill the surrounding territory had looked like an ocean of flames. I was fortunate in coming back here when I did, before the fire had spread so much, for between Columbia and Charlotte the railroad had been surrounded by burning woods at many places."

Rosalie now learned that she would enjoy the company of a Swedish family named Löwegren when she was to leave New York for England and home, and that to her great relief none of her brothers was any longer considering coming to America to find work. She could feel perfectly free to return home. From Havana, on the first leg of her circuitous journey homeward, she wrote 8 April 1855 of leaving "Dungannon": "The last days at 'Dungannon' were marked by much bustling about, but I succeeded nevertheless in getting my things into fairly good order. The trip to Cuba obliged me to supply myself in great haste with several lighter pieces of apparel. . . . The day before I left I had a party for little Anna for which I baked several kinds of cookies and made negus, which was much enjoyed by large and small. Dr. Logan and his sisters also came to say goodbye. Friday, 30 March, I left 'Dungannon' after a painful farewell all round. . . . God bless them all for the friendship they showed me! I cannot think of it without tears and being deeply moved, nor do I dare abandon myself to the thought that I shall probably never see them again. . . .

"I had hoped to meet Hulda in Charleston, but instead I only received friendly letters from her and Franz. The Legarés had persuaded her not to come, for they feared that she would feel homesick." Rosalie had also gone in to Charleston to say good-bye and to make one last visit to the Museum to "examine several of the remarkable exhibits there and to meet Professor Holmes, who promised to send at the first opportunity a box of birds to Sweden."

XII

"CHEVALIÈRE ERRANTE" IN THE NEW WORLD

Rosalie's absolute determination not to take the direct route home by boat evidently vanquished her friends' misgivings, and from them she received help of all kinds to ease her way. Letters of introduction were written to their friends and acquaintances in New Orleans, Chicago, and New York. The Swedish consul gave her a letter to his newly discovered counterpart in Havana, and the owner of a music store who had lived there for five years came to call and left with her three letters of introduction. Members of the Peronneau family arranged for her passport, money exchanges, and her steamship ticket. As she reported in her letter 4 April, a great crowd showed up for the *Isabel*'s departure to say farewell and to wish her bon voyage. "Through them I was introduced to the captain, who promised to take good care of me. . . . The day was bright and clear. I stood on deck to look back to my friends and Charleston as long as possible, but even before the city and its forts were out of sight, my old enemy, seasickness, forced me to retreat to my cabin. . . .

"At Savannah we received additions to the passenger list; however, we did not make port at that city but a steamboat came out and then they had to go through the unpleasant process of being hoisted on deck. I only want to acquaint you with those who play a part in my story and have the honor therefore of introducing Mr. and Mrs. Mickler of Easton, Pennsylvania, a young newly married couple now out on their wedding trip, and Mr. Jones, a Georgian, with black hair, beard, and bushy eyebrows, in no sense with an attractive exterior—about which person, more later. The young couple were rich and handsome and seemed disposed to enjoy and experience life's happy days; he was twenty-five years old, she twenty. She and I became very good friends and were constantly together once the seasickness permitted us to be sociable. . . .

"Among the second-class passengers was an Irish family, parents and five children, who were moving to Florida from New York, where they said it was becoming all the more difficult each year to earn a livelihood while crime and poverty were on the increase. They spoke with bitterness of the persecution their fatherland suffered at the hands of England. . . .

"Mrs. Mickler and I did not go to the table until dinner on the third day, when a champagne cork was popped in our honor. It was not until toward the end of our trip that I discovered Mr. Jones, whose name was as yet unknown to me so that I called him 'the Black Warrior'; he then began to be conversational, showed me his letters of introduction, his Spanish grammar, informed me of his travel plans, inquired after mine, etc. . . . Our trip was unusually long, and it was not until Sunday afternoon that we arrived at Havana. . . . The unusual architecture, the prodigious walls, and here and there the beautiful palms and other tropical plants make this picture one of the most romantic I have ever seen. Indeed if I were asked to speak of something truly splendid, I would merely have to say 'the harbor at Havana.'. . . We yearned to get ashore after our sea voyage, especially I, who wanted to see a Catholic service on Easter Day, but luck was against us, for a heavy squall with torrents of rain frustrated all our plans for going ashore. Feeling a little downcast, Mrs. Mickler and I sat in the captain's cabin, which was up on the deck, and stared curiously at some Spanish dignitaries who came on board to examine our papers and give us duly authorized permission to go ashore. But we had to spend yet one night more on board and feel ourselves grateful into the bargain for having been allowed to enter the harbor—had we arrived a little later, after sunset, we would have had to remain outside and probably would have been tossed about rather unceremoniously in the rough seas.

"I was on deck early the following morning to enjoy the beautiful scene—and all that I saw was splendid. . . . At last permission came to go ashore, and with it, the innkeeper at the American Hotel, who wanted to assure himself of the arrival of the passengers. As the steamship was not permitted to put in ashore, we climbed into a boat which took us to the quay and from there we walked to the city gate, in the archway of which we had to sit patiently and wait a while until the obliging customs officials (our favorites, Mama!) had looked through our baggage, which they proceeded, however, rather decently to do. It seemed to me as though we had been placed in the prisoner's dock awaiting our sentence while we sat outside an iron trellis-gate through which soldiers with swarthy complexions glared at us. I considered myself fortunate at that moment to be with Mr. and Mrs. Mickler, for otherwise my situation would have been disagreeable indeed, among barbarously strange, uncultivated persons. While the gentlemen were in the guard house to obtain further 'permits,' which cost $2, to enter the city, Mrs. Mickler and I huddled together as closely as possible. The beginning seemed to us far from propitious, and the disagreeable impression was diminished not at all when we entered the city and saw the narrow, uneven, and crooked streets, the low houses which had a ruinous appearance and because of their windows being fitted with iron bars resembled prisons, the poor little horses and donkeys which seemed ready to collapse under their burdens, and the dirty half-naked Negroes. Oh, all of Havana seemed to me like a huge prison, and I thought it impossible that one single happy creature might be found there.

"We made our way to the hotel, and after waiting a while in the large salon with its marble floor and curtains as well as jalousies instead of windows and doors, I was taken to a little dark and cramped room, the housekeeper's, which was located near the kitchen and over the stables, for which reason it had a mixture of a wide range of less than agreeable fumes. This room was the only one that was available for the time being. I had to be satisfied with accepting it and paying $3 a day or else secure other lodgings, which was then out of the question.

"After a hearty breakfast we set out on our adventures, Mr. and Mrs. Mickler, the undersigned, escorted by a flute player who was headed for California, and Mr. Jones, for whom I had already begun to feel an instinctive horror. None of us knew Spanish, and we wandered about at random looking at some churches, saw on the exterior nothing other than gray and moss-covered stone structures of a peculiar kind of architecture, while the interior consisted of a tasteless superfluity of decorations, among which silver flowers seemed to play a major role. Although it was Easter, the shops were open and all occupations seemed to proceed as on a weekday, for at the hotel I saw a Negress engaged in washing clothes. On the way home we bought magnificent oranges. I was extremely eager to have my letters of introduction delivered around in order by that means to find someone who could help set me to rights, for I felt not a little like a fish out of water in that mass of unfamiliar people. . . .

"I thought it was a shame to evict the housekeeper, an Irish girl who seemed to be of a kindly disposition, from my room; since it had two beds, I said that she could sleep there. Seldom has a little friendliness been so valued and rewarded, for Alice, that was her name, was from that day forward my friend and protectress. As she was Catholic and intended to attend mass the following day, I asked her to let me come along, and she woke me and gave me coffee at 5 in the morning, after which we walked to St. Catalina, where we remained about an hour while the mass was read and holy communion administered. The communicants themselves took the wafer, but the priest drank the wine. The priests were attired in lace shirts and over them they wore gaudy chasubles. I cannot abide their appearance."

The first impression of Havana, the "Queen of the Antilles," was, as we see, a great disappointment. In Rosalie's imagination Cuba wore the aspect of paradise, but it was not long before dream became reality, for the letters of introduction turned out to have an astonishing effect. "Monday seemed to promise to be a more pleasant day, for I had a visit before breakfast from one of my gentlemen, a Mr. de Ford. As he became one of my great favorites, I must tell you something more about him. He is happily married as of a year ago, is a handsome man about 30 years old, . . . a perfect gentleman, has traveled a great deal, lived several years in South America, most of the countries in which he has visited, has been on the slopes of the Andes and in the valleys of the Amazon, has seen all gradations from perpetual winter to perpetual summer, experienced all the variations in social life from the isolation of a wilderness where a handful of corn was a delicacy, to the sophisticated manners of civilization. And not enough with that, he is possessed of many interests and is cultivated and brought pleasure to me every day through his company.

"One ought to have plenty of time when one travels, partly in order to enjoy everything as much as possible, partly in order to make a memorandum of it, and my time hardly suffices. Let me therefore only say to you that after almost a week's visit in Havana I began to find it so agreeable, made such delightful ácquaintances, and had moreover hope of being able to make a little trip into the countryside, that I could not tear myself away when Mr. and Mrs. Mickler left but decided to stay over for another week. I did not regret this decision at all but found the time only much, much too brief. I think, however, that I could not have endured such a life any longer, for the last three days were clouded by a nasty headache, . . . but I was nevertheless out and in motion from 5 in the morning until 10 at night."

The tempo of Rosalie's days at Havana accelerated rapidly as one after the other of her new friends discovered new delights with which to please her. She was handsomely entertained by the Swedish consul John Nenninger and his wife, went sailing in the bay with a young Swede living in Havana, visited every church she could find, had her daguerreotype taken (see frontispiece), and in general enjoyed every moment of her two weeks in Cuba despite the headache of which she had complained. She confided in a letter to Hedda Hammarsköld that if she had wished it, she was sure she could have changed her name to Jones, but she was relieved to have avoided that possibility. At the end of her stay her friends arranged passage for her aboard the *Granada* bound for New Orleans and gave her a cheery send off.

She remained at New Orleans for a week. She was met there by Dr. Logan's brother Joseph, who arranged for her to live with a Creole family with whom he also boarded. He escorted her to Carrollton, where his uncle had his home, and to Lake Pontchartrain. Rosalie's impressions of Havana did not pale in comparison, but she was happy to note that she felt freer in New Orleans to move about than she had in Havana, where women, she felt, were virtual prisoners of social convention.

She set her sights next on visiting Mammoth Cave, of which she had heard much though uncertain of its exact location. It was arranged for her to travel up the Mississippi to Louisville, where she found an Englishman and his wife staying at her hotel who were themselves about to set out by diligence for the cave. His wife having decided against so strenuous an excursion after all, the Englishman by himself proved to be friendlier than Rosalie thought suitable, and yet she took great pleasure from her visit to the cave, which she explored in a Bloomer costume supplied by the local hotel. She returned to Louisville and then went on to visit some small towns in Indiana before taking passage to Cincinnati, where again letters of introduction provided her with companionship and support. She continued her journey to Chicago via Indianapolis and again had the good fortune of being assisted by a gentleman met by chance on the train who saw her safely to a hotel late at night. But she had to agree that Chicago, where Fredrika Bremer had been five years before, was just what that lady had said of it, "one of the ugliest and foulest cities in America." She reached New York by way of Detroit, Buffalo (where she made the mandatory visit to Niagara Falls), and Albany (where, inspired by an article in *Harper's Magazine*, she made an excursion to the Mountain House in the Catskills). The long visit to New York and nearby cities that she had planned for herself, now furnished with additional letters of introduction given to her by those to whom she had been thus "introduced" along the way, was cut short by the Löwegrens' decision to leave ten days early. On her last day in New York Rosalie wrote to Hedda Hammarsköld: "Today has been the first day that I have felt depressed since I began my travels. And do you know the reason why? It was sadness, sadness at leaving a part of the world where I had experienced so much goodwill, had been received with so much affection, had learned so much that is good and useful, and found peace, of which I hope I shall never be deprived."

On the *Yorkshire* Rosalie formed friendships that led as always to her being warmly received at her destination. In Liverpool she was entertained by the Swedish consul and his wife, and later she visited the botanical gardens in the company of Miss Julia Griffiths, an Englishwoman she had met aboard the *Yorkshire*. Miss Griffiths had spent six years in America as secretary of the Ladies' Anti-Slavery Society in Rochester. She was a friend and warm admirer of Frederick Douglass, the emancipated slave, and was on her way back to England to visit relatives but also to secure contributions for Douglass's magazine.[1] Rosalie was accompanied by Miss Griffiths to London, where she stayed for over three weeks. She might have sailed from there direct to Göteborg but chose instead to prolong her travels by visiting Paris for several weeks. She then made her way northward via Köln, Hamburg, and Lübeck, always falling in, it would seem, with agreeable company. The gentlemen she met were invariably models of politeness, interested in her American experiences and generous with their assistance in seeing to her baggage, transportation, and lodging. After particularly warm hospitality accorded her in Hamburg by an English-German family she had met on the train, she wrote, "It is unusual to meet people with whom one becomes so quickly acquainted and after a few hours can speak so intimately . . . and even more unusual that such an acquaintance is continued through correspondence in the same spirit, . . . these are kindred souls who meet and recognize one another without formality, without design."

She was back in Sweden by the middle of September. After a month's visit in her old home, "Sjögerås," now occupied by her married sister, she accompanied her mother to Stockholm to the house on Klarabergsgatan which her father had just finished building. She was soon in motion again, however, and journeyed to nearby Uppsala to visit Hedda Hammarsköld's two sisters there and to leave with them a full account of Hedda's life in America. In Uppsala she again met Professor Olivecrona, now a recent widower; his courtesy on this occasion suggested to her that he regretted his intemperate remarks four years before concerning her decision to travel to America. For her part, she said, her animosity "melted away like snow in April." Two years later, in June 1857, Rosalie married him; stepmother, to begin with, to four children between the ages of three and eight, in a few years' time she bore two children of her own, a daughter Eliza and a son Axel.

---

1 *The North Star*, on which Julia Griffiths had been chief editorial assistant, rescuing it from almost certain bankruptcy in its first year of existence, 1847–48. Her work with the Ladies' Anti-Slavery Society had brought her into close association with some of the leading figures in the American women's rights movement: Elizabeth Cady Stanton, Susan B. Anthony, and others. It was Mary Howitt, the English translator of Fredrika Bremer's fiction and of her *Homes of the New World* and a friend of Douglass's from the time of his visit to England in 1845–46, who had led the drive in England to provide him with funds for the purchase of a printing press. Philip S. Foner, *Frederick Douglass* (New York, 1969), pp. 76, 84. These accomplishments by women of her own time, if they arose in her conversations with Miss Griffiths, would have been of particular interest to Rosalie, who was soon to be deeply involved in social reform in Sweden.

She had returned from her years in America and her months of travel convinced, she wrote Hedda Hammarsköld in December 1855, that important, useful work lay ahead but of what kind it was still too soon for her to perceive.[2] Presumably it would in any case involve her taking the lead in some sort of reform, for she already had had opportunity to see how easily good and reasonable plans could be drawn up yet what obstacles they invariably encountered in "vested interests, petty thinking, prejudices, indolence, lack of cooperation." Encouraged by Hedda's praise of her skill as a writer, Rosalie wondered nevertheless whether it was sufficient to survive the hazards of a career as a writer. Hedda had supposed that Rosalie's gift was for poetry, but Rosalie herself, although a slim volume of her verse had been published pseudonymously on her return to Sweden, doubted that she had either the genius for poetry or even the imagination required for writing acceptable verse. One had, she wrote Hedda, only to note the sorry state into which poetry had fallen in Sweden and the brevity of the careers of promising new poets to realize what tremendous odds she would have to face. She saw that for all of Fredrika Bremer's remarkable ability and her obvious good intentions, she was constantly ridiculed by critics simply because "she is a woman and as such has had the audacity to undertake something other than sewing and has occupied herself with something other than gossip about her neighbors." Rosalie doubted that she could endure such criticism herself; it would silence her, she said, once for all. Yet she could not completely dismiss the possibility of earning fame and money through writing novels, if not verse, enough at least to win support for long cherished plans to foster the means for young girls to advance their education and make them employable.

Convinced, then, that she had a calling but uncertain what it might be, Rosalie passed an unhappy winter in her home in Stockholm after returning from America. "I ought now to be so glad, so happy, to be back among my own family, yet there is something lacking—I feel myself to be the most ungrateful of all beings. I think I would be calmer if I could discover the cause of this melancholy." She had already sought out Fredrika Bremer but with no more satisfactory result than to be sponsored by her for membership in the Women's Society for Child Care, "good work" of a kind permitted unmarried women. There was nevertheless a bright

2 The account that follows draws on the chapter entitled "Rosalie Roos" in Sigrid Leijonhufvud, *Sophie Adlersparre* (Stockholm, 1922), pp. 31–37, as supplemented and corrected by Sigrid Laurell, "Rosalie Roos och Tidskrift för hemmet," in *Kvinnolitteraturforskning: teorier och begynnelser*, ed. Karin Westman Berg and Gabriella Åhmansson (Uppsala, 1979), pp. 80–101.

spot: her growing friendship with Sophie Leijonhufvud, a woman her own age with impeccable social credentials and with an active interest in literature, the arts, and social issues. The two women attended concerts, lectures, and plays together, a welcome relief for Rosalie from the intense boredom she felt in helping her parents fulfill routine social obligations.

In 1859 she and Sophie became coeditors of *Tidskrift för Hemmet*, the newly started organ of the Swedish women's movement. Rosalie's editorial work gave her the opportunity to put some of her ideas into practice at last and to make use of her abilities as a writer both in editing and in occasionally contributing to the magazine. But working conditions were far from ideal. She had her home to manage, including the responsibility of rearing children and stepchildren and of meeting the sometimes exacting requirements of the role of a professor's wife in Uppsala; and in addition, at her husband's request she read his manuscripts before publication. Given all these demands on her time and energy, she had at first declined Sophie's suggestion that she be her coeditor. At Sophie's insistence, however, she eventually yielded, conscious also on her part that Sophie had come too recently to the profession of writing and indeed to the ideas which together they now espoused in behalf of women to be able to carry on the work of launching the *Tidskrift* alone. The coeditors had to depend chiefly on the post between Uppsala and Stockholm to reach decisions and to clear away inevitable difficulties having to do with contributors and the printer. Sophie, moreover, worked less systematically than did Rosalie, who was at times hastily pressed into service to meet deadlines for articles or for proofreading without due regard to her many other responsibilities. The magazine nevertheless prospered, but the toll on Rosalie's patience and strength proved in time to be too heavy, and over the objections even of her husband, who had helped the two women with legal questions in starting up the magazine and had in time become fully convinced of its value, she was finally permitted to withdraw at the end of the ninth year. Sophie continued alone and in 1884 helped found the Fredrika Bremer Society, which adopted *Tidskrift för Hemmet* as its organ, renaming it *Dagny*, and later *Hertha*.

Marriage, in addition to giving Rosalie the domestic milieu she thrived in, allowed her the freedom of movement so necessary to her after her sampling of it in America yet generally unavailable in those years in Sweden to unmarried women. She used it well as far as she felt propriety permitted. She and Sophie performed their editorial work anonymously, although it soon became widely known who these daring workers were. She contributed articles to magazines and newspapers, but always under a pseudonym, and only once did she appear in public as a lecturer, when she spoke late in life on the current status of the women's movement. There was less need of discretion in her promotion of handicrafts as an independent source of income for women, or in her work for the improved care and education of retarded children. Her husband's appointment to the Supreme Court in 1868 imposed a further need for tact in her activities in behalf of women's rights at a time when the subject was highly inflammatory, and perhaps for reasons of that kind she later refused the appointment offered her on the board of directors of the Fredrika Bremer Society. But as she once wrote Hedda Hammarsköld, anyone who had tasted as she had in America the fruits of independence, of earning money and of moving about on her own, would not willingly settle for anything less.

Eliza Peronneau continued to correspond with Rosalie until the latter's death on 4 June 1898. The Peronneaus lost possession of "Dungannon" in the Civil War, and Eliza's husband's plantation in Georgia was reduced to ruins. Rosalie consequently brought Eliza's young daughter Clelia to Sweden for a year's visit, and the descendants of the two families have continued to meet and to correspond to this day.